PRACTICAL SOCIAL WORK

Series Editor: Jo Campling

(BASW)

Social ork is at so important stage in its development. All
profe nsive to changing social and economic
condi meet the needs of those they serve. This
series on sound practice and the specific contribution which
social workers can make to the well-being of our society in the
1990s.

The British Association of Social Workers has always been conscious of its role in setting guidelines for practice and in seeking to
raise professional standards. The conception of the Practical Social
Work series arose from a survey of BASW members to discover
where they, the practitioners in social work, felt there was the m
need for new literature. The response was overwhelming and
enthusiastic, and the result is a carefully planned, coherent series of
books. The emphasis is firmly on practice, set in a theoretical
framework. The books will inform, stimulate and promote discussion, thus adding to the further development of skills and high
professional standards. All the authors are practitioners and teachers of social work, representing a wide variety of experience.

JO CAMPLING

005

PUBLISHED

Robert Adams *Self-Help, Social Work and Empowerment*

David Anderson *Social Work and Mental Handicap*

James G. Barber *Beyond Casework*

Peter Beresford and Suzy Croft *Citizen Involvement: A Practical Guide for Change*

Suzy Braye and Michael Preston-Shoot *Practising Social Work Law*

Robert Brown, Stanley Bute and Peter Ford *Social Workers at Risk*

Alan Butler and Colin Pritchard *Social Work and Mental Illness*

Crescy Cannan, Lynne Berry and Karen Lyons *Social Work and Europe*

Roger Clough *Residential Work*

David M. Cooper and David Ball *Social Work and Child Abuse*

Veronica Coulshed *Management in Social Work*

Veronica Coulshed *Social Work Practice: An introduction (2nd edn)*

Paul Daniel and John Wheeler *Social Work and Local Politics*

Peter R. Day *Sociology in Social Work Practice*

Lena Dominelli *Anti-Racist Social Work: A Challenge for White Practitioners and Educators*

Celia Doyle *Working with Abused Children*

Angela Everitt, Pauline Hardiker, Jane Littlewood and Audrey Mullender *Applied Research for Better Practice*

Kathy Ford and Alan Jones *Student Supervision*

David Francis and Paul Henderson *Working with Rural Communities*

Michael D. A. Freeman *Children, their Families and the Law*

Alison Froggatt *Family Work with Elderly People*

Danya Glaser and Stephen Frosh *Child Sexual Abuse*

Bryan Glastonbury *Computers in Social Work*

Gill Gorell Barnes *Working with Families*

Cordelia Grimwood and Ruth Popplestone *Women, Management and Care*

Jalna Hanmer and Daphne Statham *Women and Social Work: Towards a Woman-Centred Practice*

Tony Jeffs and Mark Smith (eds) *Youth Work*

Michael Kerfoot and Alan Butler *Problems of Childhood and Adolescence*

Joyce Lishman *Communication in Social Work*

Mary Marshall *Social Work with Old People (2nd edn)*

Paula Nicolson and Rowan Bayne *Applied Psychology for Social Workers (2nd edn)*

Kieran O'Hagan *Crisis Intervention in Social Services*

Michael Oliver *Social Work with Disabled People*

Joan Orme and Bryan Glastonbury *Care Management: Tasks and Workloads*

Malcolm Payne *Social Care in the Community*

Malcolm Payne *Working in Teams*

John Pitts *Working with Young Offenders*

Michael Preston-Shoot *Effective Groupwork*

Carole R. Smith *Adoption and Fostering: Why and How*

Carole R. Smith *Social Work with the Dying and Bereaved*

Carole R. Smith, Marty T. Lane and Terry Walsh *Child Care and the Courts*

Gill Stewart and John Stewart *Social Work and Housing*

Christine Stones *Focus on Families*

Neil Thompson *Anti-Discriminatory Practice*

Neil Thompson with Michael Murphy and Steve Stradling *Dealing with Stress*

Derek Tilbury *Working with Mental Illness*

Alan Twelvetrees *Community Work (2nd edn)*

Hilary Walker and Bill Beaumount (eds) *Working with Offenders*

Self-Help, Social Work and Empowerment

Robert Adams

MACMILLAN

First published 1990 by
THE MACMILLAN PRESS LTD
Houndmills, Basingstoke, Hampshire RG21 2XS
and London
Companies and representatives
throughout the world

ISBN 0–333–46984–4 hardcover
ISBN 0–333–46985–2 paperback

A catalogue record for this book is available
from the British Library.

Reprinted 1993, 1994

Printed in Hong Kong

Series Standing Order

If you would like to receive future titles in this series as they are published, you can
make use of our standing order facility. To place a standing order please contact your
bookseller or, in case of difficulty,write to us at the address below with your name
and address and the name of the series. Please state with which title you wish to
begin your standing order. (If you live outside the United Kingdom we may not have
the rights for your area, in which case we will forward your order to the publisher
concerned.)

Customer Services Department, Macmillan Distribution Ltd
Houndmills, Basingstoke, Hampshire RG21 2XS, England

To Winifred Adams

Contents

Preface

This book grew partly from personal experiences of the need for self-help to contribute to the care of my own relatives and partly from my efforts to support the self-help initiatives of MIND, as the then chairperson of MIND's advisory committee in Yorkshire and Humberside. To that chance initiation into the politics of empowerment in mental health I owe a debt to Norman Jepson and John Crowley. Through involvement in Mind Your Self in Leeds, my collaboration with Gael Lindenfield, who founded it, led to several books and other publications.

The book began partly also with the awareness that despite the growing numbers of handbooks on self-help, there was a need for an accessible yet critical text, which would provide a framework for the development of more effective relationships between professionals and self-helpers.

Several years later, during study leave from the College, I started to write on the basis of a series of visits to a wide variety of self-help groups and organisations throughout the UK. I should like to record my appreciation to the many people to whom, in the process, I spoke about the subject matter of this book. The list is too long to mention everyone here, but thanks are due in any case to Helen Allison, Mike Archer, Don Barton, David Brandon, Francis Conway, Gilly Craddock, Dave Crenson, Parul Desai, Nick Ellerby, John Errington, Alec Gosling, John Hannan, Gerry Lynch, Peter McGavin, Sam McTaggart, Jim Pearson, Tom Rhodenberg, Alan Robinson, Gill Thorpe, Bob Welburn and Tom Woolley. I am particularly grateful also to Dorothy Whitaker and Terence O'Sullivan for their comments on earlier drafts of this book, and to Paddy Hall for his ideas on community education.

Part of the process of production has been based at home, I have to acknowledge that my own household has seen its share of debates about self-help and empowerment over the past eighteen months and many improvements to the text have resulted from these. So, particular thanks are due to Pat, Charlotte, Kirsty, Jade and George.

Finally, I am learning as I write how valuable is the guidance and support of a good editor. For her encouragement and patience at the critical stages, my thanks go to Jo Campling.

It goes without saying, but needs saying of course, that, whilst much of the content of the book reflects the various contributions of those mentioned, among many others, all the opinions expressed in it, and any errors, are entirely my own.

ROBERT ADAMS

List of Abbreviations

AA	Alcoholics Anonymous
ACC	Association of County Councils
AIDS	Acquired Immune-deficiency Syndrome
Al-Anon	Organisation for relatives and friends of people with a drink problem
AMA	Association of Metropolitan Authorities
ARC	Asian Resources Centre, Birmingham
BASW	British Association of Social Workers
CARE	Cancer Aftercare and Rehabilitation Society
CCETSW	Central Council for Education and Training in Social Work
CVS	Council for Voluntary Service
CR	Consciousness-raising
DHSS	Department of Health and Social Security
GMHC	Gay Men's Health Crisis
NCVO	National Council for Voluntary Organisations
PSHPG	Peer Self-help Psychotherapy Groups
RSSPCC	Royal Scottish Society for the Prevention of Cruelty to Children
SCF	Save the Children Fund
THT	Terrence Higgins Trust
WHO	World Health Organisation

1

Self-Help: A Case of Unfair Dismissal

Introduction

What is self-help and how does it relate to social work and empowerment? 'Self-help' may be defined as a process, group or organisation comprising people coming together or sharing an experience or problem, with a view to individual and/or mutual benefit. As empowerment commonly means 'becoming powerful', self-help may thus be viewed as one form of empowerment. Through self-help, as we shall see below, social workers and self-helpers can empower others and be empowered themselves. Though the main focus of this book is on self-help and social work, its purpose is empowerment.

Every social worker has come into contact at one time or another with self-help activities as defined above. But, all too often, there is a tendency for the social worker to view self-help as simply nothing to do with social work at all. Or, self-help becomes a political football, kicked about by opposing political factions, regarded from the Left as a justification for cuts in health and social services and from the Right as the route to prosperity.

The difficulty is that at first sight the two areas of self-help and social work seem to be incompatible. To caricature the position, socialist social workers may tend to dismiss self-help as a potentially destructive irrelevance while the more conservative use it as an excuse for opting out. Either way, the territory of self-help activities gets less attention from social workers than it deserves. The argument of this book is that this tendency to dismiss self-help

1

– or at least to shy away from engaging positively with self-help activities – is at best wasteful of resources and at worst downright counterproductive.

At the same time that the field of self-help receives less constructive attention than it deserves, the related notion of empowerment is taking off. Empowerment has come of age in the late 1980s. This may complicate the discussion of self-help, but it offers considerable liberating potential for social work practice. Of course, empowerment is a concept which is larger than the focus of this book, it demands examination in a larger arena. But this should not inhibit us from referring to it here, as a means of empowering both self-helpers and social workers themselves.

So the fact that the character of self-help needs clarifying and the relationship between self-help and social work sorting out, should not put social workers off. But if the decision to engage with self-help is to be empowering, it needs to be purposeful. The task of this book is to provide social workers with a framework for that purposeful practice. It sets out a basis for competence in dealing with the self-help field, assuming that competence in practice rests on a combination of understanding, knowledge and skills in an appropriate context of values. In tackling this, the first task is to clarify the concept of self-help, before going on to examine how social workers relate to self-help in a variety of ways in different settings.

Chapters 1 and 2 examine the nature of self-help, and set out a framework for relating it to social work practice. Chapters 3–5 deal specifically with the three major ways in which social workers relate to self-help activity. More than that, they draw attention to the steps which need to be taken to ensure the effectiveness of such practice. In Chapters 6–9 we take up issues which apply generally to the entire self-help field.

What is self-help?

The scope of 'self-help' is much broader than just social work. Health and social services apart, contemporary self-help includes such fields as agricultural self-sufficiency, alternative communities and communes and worker participation in industry (Stokes, 1981, pp. 18–19), most of which are not relevant to social work and this book.

The constantly changing variety of practice

The great variety and ever-changing character of self-help activity makes it difficult to pin down its essential characteristics. Groups are coming into existence and disappearing all the time. In fact, Levy has noted that they change so quickly that a static directory of them is not much use (Levy, 1982, p. 1267). Yet there is a continuity in views of the idea of self-help, which stands independent of the vulnerability or short life of particular groups.

There is great variety also in the levels at which people get involved in self-help and in the focus of activities. There is a common belief that self-help is simply about a few people getting together in a small group for a meeting concerning their shared problems. While groups are an important aspect of self-help, it is also true that many self-help activities are initiated by individuals in respect of themselves. Furthermore, some communities get involved in self-help. The area of self-help varies from problem-focusing through self-development to consciousness raising.

Problem-focusing

Problem-focusing activities range from people's efforts to help themselves and each other with health problems such as eating disorders or substance abuse, mental health problems such as depression and phobias and social problems such as loneliness. They include anonymous groups, relatives' and carers' groups, therapy groups and groups for people experiencing stigma.

Anonymous groups   There is an ever-expanding list of groups modelling themselves on Alcoholics Anonymous (AA), the largest, most well known and probably the oldest of them all. They include Cancer Anonymous, Checks Anonymous, Convicts Anonymous, Crooks Anonymous, Delinquents Anonymous, Disturbed Children Anonymous, Divorcees Anonymous, Dropouts Anonymous, Fatties Anonymous, Gamblers Anonymous, Migraines Anonymous, Mothers Anonymous, Narcotics Anonymous, Neurotics Anonymous, Parents Anonymous, Parents of Youth in Trouble Anonymous, Prison Families Anonymous, Psychotics Anonymous, Recidivists Anonymous, Relatives Anonymous, Retirees Anonymous, Rich Kids Anonymous, Schizophrenics Anonymous, Sexual Child Abusers Anonymous, Skin Anonymous, Smokers Anonymous, Stutterers Anonymous, Suicide Anonymous and Youth Anonymous (Gartner and Riessman, 1977, p. 25).

Well-established groups such as AA tend to have clearly specified principles covering their meetings and rules for members. AA displays in a form relatively unchanged since its founding in 1935, a number of principles, many of which are found also in other anonymous groups, including 'the focus on behaviour; the attention to symptoms; the importance of the role of the group and the value of the knowledge and experience of the "oldtimers" [long-time members]; and the viewing of the problem [alcoholism] as chronic [the alcoholic is viewed as never being cured]' (Gartner and Riessman, 1977, p. 25). The controlling tendencies of Alcoholics Anonymous – mutual surveillance by members and public concern about, if not actual punishment of, backsliders – are found in many other Anonymous groups. Such groups are concerned invariably with working within accepted societal norms to change the behaviour of individuals. In AA the individual is expected to be guided by the Twelve Steps and the Twelve Traditions.

The fact that the ideology of AA has found its way into several of the other larger Anonymous organisations is not surprising because Gamblers Anonymous, Narcotics Anonymous and Neurotics Anonymous were founded by members of AA and have accepted the Twelve Steps and the Twelve Traditions on which their work is based (Gartner and Riessman, 1977, p. 29–31).

Groups for relatives and carers   Many groups have been set up in recent years to deal with the special circumstances and difficulties which can arise for people who are living with somebody who has a problem. In these cases, self-help groups offer an indirect form of support for those with problems, through the help given directly to the carer, who may be a friend or a relative.

The group may run in partnership with an existing group which caters directly for the person experiencing the problem. An example is Al-Anon, for relatives and friends of someone with a drink problem, who may be a member of an AA group. The nature of this sort of support group, sometimes called a 'living-with group', is affected greatly by the extent of dependence on the carer of the person with the problem. The care of an elderly confused relative who is doubly incontinent, or for a baby, may have to cope with a much greater intensity of round-the-clock involvement in the task and the impact on her or him may be much greater.

The living-with group quite often caters for members trying to cope with people who have similar conditions. Initial contact with such a group is likely to provide the newcomer with the reassurance of meeting someone who has been through the same, or very similar, conditions before. It will probably also provide her or him with much needed information about the condition, from the standpoint of the carer. Parents who get together because they have children suffering from the same illness may thus share experiences, from their first awareness that something was wrong, to the present day.

Self-help therapy groups   There is a vast variety of self-help groups with a therapeutic orientation. However, it is in the area of feminist therapy groups that some of the most exciting, and paradoxical features of self-help can be seen. Feminist therapy reflects the influence of feminism on psychotherapy and unsurprisingly its principal focus is on the impact of sexism on the problems of individual women. Importantly, the attention is paid to sexism as one aspect of the social structure (Howell, 1981, p. 512). To that extent, feminist therapy no less than much psychotherapy acknowledges the social dimension of problems which seem to be located within the individual.

The feminist therapy group may be represented as one type of consciousness-raising. But to the extent that consciousness-raising is concerned with social and political – or at any rate extra-psychic – change, the activity of therapy may be absent from it altogether (Howell, 1981, p. 510). With regard to feminist therapy groups, a more subtle and challenging issue emerges. If we accept that fundamental to the feminist viewpoint is the preoccupation with the socially- rather than individually-based explanation of a person's symptoms, then the likelihood is that the feminist will regard as suspect any hint that the causes of a problem lie in individual pathology. We may thus find that feminist therapy which rejects psychodynamic discussion of the origins of, and responses to, problems resembles consciousness-raising since it is likely to assert the need for social change and political action.

Groups for people experiencing stigma   AA is but one expression of an enthusiasm for self-help which has a fervour drawn in part from moral crusades to improve the lot of the unfortunate. In the politicisation of AIDS we can detect a hardening of attitudes towards the victim of the condition, which perhaps heightens the moralistic tone of official responses. But the self-help groups and organisations which grew in response to AIDS differ from AA. Whereas AA itself has taken on some of the moral values of society in relation to drink problems, self-help AIDS groups, if anything, set themselves against such moral attitudes.

In the 1980s, AIDS has become a focus of self-help activity. In a way, this illustrates a tendency of governments and officials to push the responsibility for developing the condition onto individuals. AIDS tends to be perceived as a consequence of the lifestyle of the individual rather than as a matter of public health. AIDS is seen as the 'gay plague'. Implicitly, there is an assumption that to catch AIDS is to demonstrate perverted or immoral habits, such as homosexuality or promiscuousness.

Taken in the context of a general tendency for government to contract public health services to private entrepreneurs and to encourage self-help in the context of an enhanced voluntary sector, it is not surprising that self-help is growing in the AIDS field. More important, perhaps, this is an illustration of the role self-help plays in areas of life where prejudice and moral panics rule over tolerance and rationality.

In the US, the most well-known self-help organisation, New York Gay Men's Health Crisis (GMHC), was founded in 1981 by forty men whose friends or lovers had AIDS. Although its members sought services to help them, they seem to have found soon that they had to get on and help themselves (Altman, 1986, p. 84). In 1982, the AIDS Foundation developed from its base in California into a national organisation, involved in educational and lobbying activities (Altman, 1986, p. 88). In general, in countries where gay organisations flourish and have strong links with government, AIDS self-help has tended to develop around them. This has happened in Canada, Denmark and the Netherlands. In Britain also, after Terrence Higgins died from AIDS, the Terrence Higgins Trust (THT) was founded in 1982, modelled largely on the GMHC. By mid-1985, the THT had over 250 volunteers (Altman, 1986, p. 91). Gay organisations have mobilised and grown in strength around health issues such as AIDS in much the same way that many feminist groups have focused upon issues concerned with women's health. But this does not mean that self-help is the preserve exclusively of gay groups, or of men or women. Yet it is a reflection of the way AIDS has had an impact on the gay community, by increasing its cohesion and solidarity.

The growth of groups like Sexual Compulsives Anonymous, Excessives Anonymous, Sex Anonymous (in New York), Sex and Love Addicts Anonymous (in San Francisco, Los Angeles and Boston) (Altman, 1986, p. 159), illustrates a growing movement towards self-help with what are perceived as sexual problems.

Self-development

Self-development includes a wide variety of activities with an educational, social and personal development focus, including Peer Self-Help Psychotherapy Groups and Integrity Groups (PSHPG) which have spread widely throughout the US. It also includes a great range of gender-associated health groups in Britain.

Peer Self-Help Psychotherapy Groups may or may not be affiliated to the national newtork of the same name and their local practices, such as frequency of meeting, vary widely. Their focus varies also, from quite major shared problems of addiction or neurosis to the general concern of personal development. It has been noted that these groups are not without a number of the difficulties which beset self-help groups generally; the development of cliques, disruption to groups activities by individual members who are feeling upset or disturbed, exploitation of the lonely and distressed by predatory group members and the reinforcement of problems by an over-emphasis on problems and bad experiences in meetings (Hurvitz, 1974, p. 93). As Hurvitz says: 'Most people with a problem that defines a particular group never attend a PSHPG meeting, despite the considerable publicity some of these groups receive' (1974, p. 92).

Integrity Groups exemplify the way some such activities cross the boundary between problem-focusing and self-development. Integrity Groups operate in the US and illustrate a well-established and structured approach to self-help in mental health. The groups run according to detailed guidelines which are open enough to allow a variety of practice. Members have to commit themselves to three principles: honesty, responsibility and involvement in group proceedings.

Gender-associated groups   Although the women's movement is particularly visible and influential in the field of self-help and health, this is not to suggest that the issue of gender should be addressed only in that area. Clearly, gender issues affect the entire field of self-help. Though women self-helpers may be described as benefiting from the support offered by a group, this is an experience many men also seek.

The nature of gender-linked groups has been influenced by feminism and by the way the women's movement has highlighted the oppression of women in general, in the workplace, the home, education, leisure and other activities. It also confronts gender inequalities in the practice of professionals such as doctors, teachers and social workers. It is unavoidable that challenges by women to the masculine biases in the study of culture and society (Rowbotham, 1980, p. 55), and in the power relations which reflect them, tend to be reflected by the illustrations in this section coming from women's groups. This should not be regarded complacently as inevitable or proper, but as one sign of male power over the everyday construction of, and talk about, self-help.

Gender-associated groups illustrate the impossibility of segregating self-help activities concerned with problems or self-development from the concerns of consciousness-raising. Women's groups include those concerned with health, therapy and consciousness-raising. However, some women writing about Women's Liberation Groups distinguish these from therapy groups, by the fact that the latter promote solutions to the problems of individual women while the former argue that such solutions for individual women depend first on changes in the conditions in which all women live their lives (Zweig, 1971, p. 161).

Health groups   Health groups may be viewed by members of educating them out of their socialisation into professionally dominated situations. Groups may set out to reveal ways in which the health professions shelter behind displays of professional knowledge and skill. They have resurrected a public approach to health rather than a private contract to cure (Chamberlain, 1981, p. 155). Groups may thus be able to resist dominant societal attitudes and may act politically to tackle health issues.

Women's health groups are concerned more broadly with the struggle for autonomy, the right to choose, make decisions and exercise control over what happens to their bodies. Women's health groups typically comprise eight or nine members meeting regularly to exchange experiences and knowledge about their bodies, feelings, attitudes and problems. While members discuss some matters of particular concern to women, such as pregnancy, menstruation and some cancers, they may be concerned also with more general health issues. Women's health groups may well be based on holistic principles, having regard to a person's needs in relation to the entire environment.

Consciousness-raising (CR)

This may focus on benefit to the individual, but in such settings as women's health groups or community action groups may take on a social change character. To the extent that feminist therapy reflects the influence of feminism on psychotherapy, the concern of such groups is partly problem-focused and partly on sexism as one aspect of the social structure (Howell, 1981, p. 512). Self-help groups involving women cover a wide range of areas from specific gynaecological topics to general health or consciousness-raising. However, Marieskind's point that most are primarily educational and concerned with enabling individuals to realise their potential (Marieskind, 1984, p. 28), should not deflect our attention from the tensions between problem-focused and consciousness-raising self-help activities.

Survivors' groups　Survivors' groups form a powerful and growing force in the field of mental health reform. But in the fields of mental health, handicap and disability, it is still all too easy for professionals and carers to take over and do people's participating and self-helping for them. One illustration of the upsurge of consumer-led self-advocacy is the growth of 'Survivors Speak Out'. Survivors' groups have spread through the developed countries and include former patients, such as people who have been in mental hospitals. Some have well-established networks of contact people, furthered in some cases by magazines or newsletters. Survivors Speak Out is a network founded in 1985 in Britain, which helps individuals and groups to keep in touch with each other and encourages self-advocacy.

Self-advocacy   Self-advocacy is becoming increasingly important in some fields of self-help, notably mental health. It is a term which refers to some initiatives in the direction of consumerism (to which, along with survivors' groups, we return in Chapter 5). Co-operatives for people with physical and mental handicaps, linked with self-advocacy, are becoming more common as people seek more imaginative ways of promoting self-help among those experiencing a range of disabilities.

In general, the significance of the latter developments reflects the way such moves as attempts to move towards the democratisation of social work services have helped to give social workers the impetus to explore ways of working alongside consumer groups in the health and social services in recent years. This is partly as a result of the growing strength of consumer-led movements generally. One result has been a trend towards some professionals acknowledging that many people have the capacity to do things for themselves, but need empowering in order to achieve them.

The essential elements of consciousness-raising in the self-help field which are worth noting at this stage include their critical stance in relation to the services they receive, and the innovative and (from the viewpoint of the bureaucrat) the often untidy and unruly character of groups and organisations. Yet, as we shall see in Chapter 5, this is the vital, energising and creative force which gives this area of self-help so much of its momentum, from which social workers have so much to learn and to gain.

An essentially neutral concept

Despite what has just been said, it may seem paradoxical to assert here that 'self-help' is essentially a neutral descriptive term which has acquired significance through the historical and social context in which it has become popular. Political judgements made by commentators about what sort of health and social work services are desirable affect their views about self-help itself. To one person, it may be seen as a highly attractive option, whilst to another it represents an unattractive consequence of the contracting Welfare State. On one hand, it appears ideal, on the other hand, it represents anathema.

This was true in the past also. Samuel Smiles, writing in mid-Victorian England, saw self-help as an expression of individualism, since it denotes activities whereby individuals and small groups deal with their problems (Smiles, 1890). The role of professionals is largely limited to exhorting people to pull themselves up by their own bootstraps, with a little material and spiritual support for those whose efforts prove they deserve it. In contrast, Kropotkin (1902) writing before the Russian Revolution, saw the collective benefits of self-help, the goal being a nationally healthy community, aiming to fulfil the individual and provide insurance against people's loss of control over their own lives by improving their participation in the local community. In addition, he felt that self-help should set out to improve the self-awareness of individuals.

Problems of definition

There is also a lack of consensus in contemporary definitions of self-help. Some commentators emphasise self-help in groups and in the community, whilst others talk as though self-help is purely associated with the efforts of individuals. Katz and Bender's definition of self-help as group activity is a good starting point. They say that self-help groups are

> voluntary small group structures for mutual aid in the accomplishment of a specific purpose. They are usually formed by peers who have come together for mutual assistance in satisfying a common need, overcoming a common handicap or life-disrupting problem, and bringing about desired social and/or personal change (Katz and Bender, 1976, p. 9).

In the medical context, Michael Moeller (1983, p. 69) suggests that self-help groups have six characteristics:

- All members are equal in status
- Each makes decisions for herself or himself
- The group is responsible for its own decisions
- Each member joins because of her or his own problems
- Group proceedings are confidential
- Participation is free.

Knight and Hayes (1981, Chapter 2) identify at least seven characteristics of self-help: voluntary activity, members having shared problems, meetings for mutual benefit, sharing of the roles of helper and helped, constructive action towards shared goals, groups run by members and groups existing without outside funding. Pancoast's definition locates self-help as a kind of counterpoint, running alongside, complementary with, formally provided services (Pancoast *et al.*, 1983, p. 19).

Integral self-help as described in Chapter 3 below is difficult to reconcile with the simple statement that self-help necessarily is independent of all outside funding. What is more crucial, perhaps, in this book concerned with social work, is the need to clarify the relationship between self-helpers and professionals. Many are prepared to admit that professional guidance may play a legitimate part in self-help activity, though the structure and mode of operation must be under members' control. 'This definition thus rules out agency-sponsored and professionally led therapy groups as well as proprietary groups such as Weight-Watchers. But it includes such groups as Parents Without Partners and Parents Anonymous, which may either utilise professional advisory committees or include referral to professionals among their ways of helping their members, when this seems indicated' (Levy, 1976, p. 306). However, self-help can be distinguished from other forms of helping in that self-helpers help themselves without recourse to professional social workers. That is, in the process of self-help they are not treated, given therapy, counselled or otherwise put into the situation of clients of social workers.

In a literature review, a very useful list of self-help characteristics has been identified: members sharing a common experience; mutual help and support; the helping of peers by those normally on the receiving end of help themselves; differential association by which people who wish to change decide to join groups in which existing members reinforce desired behaviour; collective willpower and belief in that group values emphasise the fact that change is within members' capacities; information about what experiences and changes are likely to be encountered by a member of a group; and finally the use of activities as a constructive occurrence which members share in pursuing planned goals (Killilea, 1976, pp. 67–73).

A difficulty with Killilea's description is that it concentrates on groups and the implication is that activities focus on reinforcing desired behaviour and change in individual participants. Clearly, self-help occurs at different levels and focuses on other aspects besides people's problems. A further complication is the need to make reference to the relationship between professional helpers like social workers and the self-help field. Undoubtedly, social work and self-help are complementary in some aspects, but in others self-help may function as an alternative to – or actually in conflict with – professional values.

What do self-helpers do?

The answer to this question provides a simple way of classifying self-help. For instance, among self-help health groups we can distinguish those providing direct services from those concerned with ancillary activities such as research, education or pressure activities. The latter are likely to be older established and more secure, while the former are more loosely organised, informal and with small or non-existent operating budgets (Tracy and Gussow, 1976, p. 382).

To try to be more systematic, it is useful to break down the range of self-help activities in more detail. Five kinds of activity may be identified: therapeutic, social, educational, community action and research.

Therapeutic

The range of therapeutic activities is very wide and covers an equally wide variety of medical, remedial and social work areas. The emphasis is on facilities and treatments which either complement existing ones or act as alternatives.

Social

The generation of social activities is an unsurprising feature of those groups and organisations where people meet regularly. The provision of refreshments and outings often counterpoints the primary declared purposes of groups and organisations.

Educational

Usually, educational activities are directed at external individuals or agencies with the aim of raising their level of knowledge and awareness in the field covered by a particular group or organisation. Professionals may be a target, but participants may also want to inform each other and members of the general public. Courses, workshops and conferences may be organised in the more ambitious programmes.

Community action

The self-help movement has the capacity to innovate and express activist sentiments. Working in Chicago before the Second World War, Saul Alinsky produced an approach to community action, exemplified by the Industrial Areas Foundation (Vattano, 1972, p. 12). Further, in Chicago in 1967, a gang of black youths called the Mighty Blackstone Rangers developed a degree of control over community disorder which ensured that their district of Woodlawns had no trouble. Other gangs in Negro districts in other parts of the US pursued a similar policy. In Nathan Caplan's study of riots in Detroit, he suggests that the interest the rioter and the anti-rioter both have in civil disorder brings them closer together than either is to the non-rioter (Dumont, 1971, p. 152–3). These examples highlight a feature of self-help – namely, that it tends to lie close to the way particular people experience the problems with which they are grappling.

Research

Some of the more established self-help organisations may, as indicated by Tracy and Gussow above, reach a point where public funds are allocated to research that they direct or co-ordinate. This research may have the aim of benefiting individuals suffering from a particular condition, or may serve the function of promoting pressure group activity or a community action campaign.

How do we view the process of self-help?

Three stages seem to be common to most of the self-help activities we have discussed above: initiation, self-movement and prosely-tising.

Initiation

Initiation or entry entails starting an activity or breaking into an existing one. A variety of significant elements may be associated with the start of the self-help process, to do with the preparations an individual makes, such as admitting that an issue or problem has reached the point where something needs to be done about it. At this point, the person may desire to join a group or find someone with whom to share the experience. During this period a new group may be set up, or an agreement may be reached between a new member and an existing group, about how the group may be useful and what she or he may bring to it.

Self-movement

The idea of self-movement is used here to include a wide range of activities, all of which involve a self-sustaining element. This may be problem-centred, socialisation or growth-centred, self-development or training-centred, consciousness-raising or social action-centred.

We can be more specific. For instance, in the problem-centred and problem-solving areas, the focus may be upon *change*. Change may be anticipated at different levels and is not confined to intrapersonal change. It may involve conversion or healing, what Sarbin and Adler (1971, p. 606) call the annihilation and reconstruction of the self. Or, less melodramatically, certain behaviour may cease and other behaviour take its place. Conversion may be stimulated by trigger mechanisms, or by the use of a structure such as the public confession which forms a part of many problem-focused self-help groups. This happens in a good many of the anonymous groups modelled on AA, but it may be present also in the personal statement required of a member of a consciousness-raising group. Healing, or some other form of help, may be made available to an individual by other members of the group by means of mechanisms like acceptance. Acceptance may sound akin to forgiveness, although as happens in AA groups, healing may lie a long way from the self-reliance or mutual aid of other groups, in that in AA, responsibility for healing and forgiveness is located with God as ultimate, extra-group authority. Again, the cost of cure may be seen in quasi-religious terms to involve some act of penance, as may happen in AA.

Proselytising

In a further – possibly final – proselytising stage, the individual moves on to help others. It is a mistake to see this as necessarily following conversion, since there are circumstances where a person experiences the transition from one to the other and back again, several times. Or the two processes of helping others and being helped may proceed simultaneously. Finally, of course, a person may look outside the group and may even advertise the positive impact of the experience by recruiting others, or may leave the activity to start a fresh one.

People in different situations encounter very different issues as they go through the process of self-help. Thus, members of Weightwatchers may be able to share their successes proudly with others, whereas members of more stigmatised groups may feel driven to be more circumspect. In the latter case, members of AA may share similar problems of re-acceptance by others as some former mental patients. In the past, AA has tried to counter this by using the allergy concept of alcoholism, which assumes that people develop drink problems because of a physiological predisposition over which they have no control. In this way, AA members could be viewed as sick rather than as mentally ill or as blameworthy. One consequence could be that the presumption that the drinker is merely an allergic victim of alcohol may lead simply to the eventual release of the non-drinker from the deviant label of alcoholic. Or, the outcome could be that problem drinking becomes seen as behaviour over which some people have no control.

In contrast, the experience of a consciousness-raising group is likely to be more educational than problem-focused:

> A CR group decides to look at the topic of education. From the discussion of their personal experiences the women learn that many of them were interested in the sciences but were not encouraged to pursue their interest. They go on to look at how the fields of science are dominated by men who were actively encouraged at school to continue

their education. The women learn something about the limits imposed by sex-role stereotyping in education (Donnan and Lenton, 1985, p. 17).

What values underlie self-help activity?

Whilst at first sight the dominant approach to self-help may seem to buttress an individualistic view of social policy and a right-wing political stance, in fact groups and organisations adopt and reflect a wide range of perspectives from reactionary to radical.

According to Gartner and Riessman (1977, pp. 13–14), the philosophy of self-help is 'much more activist, consumer centred, informal, open and inexpensive'. It emphasises aprofessional themes: 'the concrete, the subjective, the experiential and the intuitive – in contrast to the professional emphasis on distance, perspective, reflection, systematic knowledge and understanding'. This clearcut division is not one many self-helpers would accept, since many are committed to the latter view. But it is worthwhile trying to set out areas of values shared by much of the self-help field. There are five recurrent themes: self-management; empowerment; anti-bureaucracy; co-operation; common experiences.

Self-management

This theme involves both an attachment to the desirability of small groups of people in face-to-face settings, or networks of postal contacts which can be managed from home, and the belief in problem management. In most self-help groups and organisations, there is a belief in the importance of participants having the skills to manage their own self-help, whether this be self-management, group leadership or whatever.

Empowerment

In fact, although in many countries people engaged in self-help would say they have been involved in empowering people for years, the actual term empowerment is one which in Britain has arrived only recently. It is increasingly common to find social workers who want to get involved in self-help activities who believe strongly in the principle of people moving towards improving their control over their circumstances. In Britain, the 1989 BASW study course linked with the Annual General Meeting, focused on empowerment and social work. This may seem to be non-controversial since a number of helping professions including social workers would subscribe to the idea of giving people more power over their lives. But first of all, many self-helpers would object to the implication that empowerment may involve professionals handing over power and second, some stigmatised groups such as gays, AIDS sufferers and schizophrenics may look to self-help as a liberation movement and this may complicate their relationships with professionals.

Anti-bureaucracy

Self-help groups and organisations often assert the need to develop ways of organising themselves which are different to many of the organisations with which they have come into contact as clients. There is thus often an emphasis on avoiding hierarchical and bureaucratic patterns of organisation.

Co-operation

The emphasis on mutual help or joint care (Wilson, 1988), which distinguishes much self-help activity from selfish individualism, is often expressed in a belief in democracy, equality of status and power within groups and organisations, shared leadership and co-operation in decision-making. Some self-help initiatives have much in common with co-operatives.

Common experiences

Quite often a requirement of participants is a willingness to start from the common base of experience defined by the group or organisation. This can involve members of a group necessarily sharing issues or problems. It also implies a resistance to internal divisions in groups between expert and lay members, therapists and clients. Although some self-help actually espouses anti-professionalism, this is not always the case. What is more often held to is the principle that self-help process should not simply be the property of professionals but should be able to be initiated and engaged in by any of the participants. On the whole, research suggests that self-help groups tend to accept rather than reject relationships with professionals (Lieberman and Borman, 1979, p. 407), whilst at the same time self-help may involve a profound critique of professional activities (Gartner and Riessman, 1977, p. 12).

The popularity of self-help

In one sense, self-help has always been popular. Although as Tax has pointed out (Tax, 1976, p. 448), self-help activity is probably as old as the history of people living in communities, in Britain it is viewed by many people as one creation of the 1979 incoming Conservative Government, or as an import from the self-help boom in the US, which has gathered pace over the past fifty years. More recently, while self-help groups may be seen simply as a perpetuation of long-established, or even prehistoric forms of mutual aid, it is more accurate perhaps to regard them as midway between such traditional 'folk' activities and fully professional services (Killilea, 1976, p. 47).

One reason that self-help attracts such criticism from left-wing politicians and others is that, in Britain at least, for 150 years or more it has often reflected the values of middle-class society. Just over a century ago, Samuel Smiles put forward essentially a bourgeois view. From his respectable middle-class position, he preached that 'poverty often purifies, and braces a man's morals' (Smiles, 1875, p. 361). The harmful vice of charity was expressed in mere giving, which contrasted with the more considered charity of useful philanthropy (Smiles, 1875, p. 324). Hard work provided the preferred route to overcoming poverty, through self-denial, thrift, individual self-improvement and self-denying economy:

> The spirit of self-help is the root of all genuine growth in the individual; and, exhibited in the lives of many, it constitutes the true source of national vigour and strength (Smiles, 1890, p. 1).

The positive aspect of these ideas is that self-help still has a place in the tradition of philanthropy and voluntary action in Britain and that the movement did not die with the end of the nineteenth century. The negative feature is the persistent tendency of individualism in social policy to propose self-help as a substitute for social work rather than as complementary with, or supplementary to, it.

Self-help and voluntary action

In the past half century, in Britain at least, self-help has gained from the increased strength of the voluntary movement. But it should be noted that although self-help involves voluntary activity, it is not synonymous with the voluntary sector.

The enthusiasm for the Welfare State after the 1940s did not see the demise of self-help. In fact, the 1950s witnessed the growth of many self-help and pressure groups. A significant report on the roles of volunteers at the end of the 1960s (Aves, 1969) strengthened the base of the voluntary sector, which still provides the support and encouragement for many self-help initiatives.

But although voluntarism was gaining in strength from the 1960s, it was a further decade before the Wolfenden Report (1978) set the tone for the renewed emphasis specifically on self-help which has gathered momentum in Britain since then. Wolfenden emphasised the significance of the voluntary sector in developing partnerships between individuals, informal networks of support, voluntary bodies themselves and the statutory agencies.

Perspectives on the growth of self-help

How can the present popularity of self-help be explained? Among the different commentaries on the growing fashion for self-help in the social work field in the developed countries, we can identify four main perspectives, developed partly in the light of the useful compendium of explanations reviewed by Lieberman and Borman (1976).

Traditionalist   According to this conservative view of history, self-help has always been there, since people first lived together, and remains essentially the same now as always. This is because it is a natural way in which people act together, outside the bonds of the family, village or tribe. From this standpoint, the only additional curiosity is the modern tendency for such groups to focus on deviance and problem-solving, in contrast with eighteenth century friendly societies.

Functionalist From this viewpoint, a number of factors have coalesced to bring about the sorts of changes in society, to which self-help activity is more or less an automatic response. That is, self-help arises naturally between the gaps left by existing services and complements them to complete the pattern of overall provision. Self-help is thus an inevitable consequence of the inability, or unwillingness, of professionals and their agencies to meet needs.

Liberal This view is located within a set of developmental evolutionary assumptions about the onward march of progress in society as a whole, and in social work in particular. Within this, a number of factors are identified which have stimulated the mushrooming of self-help among many other initiatives. According to this view, self-help may be seen in relation to a professionalised view of what will meet people's needs. Self-help thus offers an alternative to existing services, and it grows because need is inadequately or incorrectly met, rather than because it is unmet.

There is a version of this perspective which perceives the growth of interest in self-help wholly or largely in relation to some prior state provision or policy. If not actually laying responsibility at the door of governments, some commentators have attempted to explain the strengthening of self-help in terms of social policy and politics. Pancoast *et al.* (1983) identifies three factors: first, social policy responses by recent governments to some of the economic shocks of the 1970s and 1980s have undermined the case for making the State the first report for health and social care and have demoralised professional providers; second, the call for more local democracy has occurred at a time when it is actually being undermined; third, the social context has become more politicised, as is evident in the growth of civil rights, consumers' and women's movements.

In Britain, the argument that it is Conservative Government policy since 1979 which has led largely to self-help's growing popularity hardly takes account of the wider international social and political context. The growing popularity of self-help activity since the Second World War in some industrialised countries, notably Britain and the US, has been attributed to the need for other groups to supplement the nuclear family, given the decline of the extended family through the stresses of greater population mobility, urbanisation and industrialisation (Katz, 1970, p. 53). However, this thesis does not square with the well-established critique of the view that the extended family has actually declined (Laslett, 1983, p. 91).

Radical   But the emphasis in self-help on consumerism, democratisation and empowerment offers a critique of the form as well as the content of existing social policies and services. Some commentators, for this and other reasons, have located reasons for the growing prominence of self-help in more broadly based societal factors. According to Sidel and Sidel (1976, p. 67), self-help and mutual aid have arisen because of technological development, depersonalised and dehumanised institutions, the alienation of people from communities, institutions, each other and themselves, and the professionalisation of services previously carried out informally by people for themselves or others. Gartner and Riessman add to much the same argument that the self-help movement has received stimulus more recently from the values of the 1960s, namely 'the concern for personal autonomy, participation, quality of life, human potential, consumer rights, deprofessionalisation and decentralisation' (Gartner and Riessman, 1977, pp. 3–4). In fact, self-help may be seen as a response to widespread alienation in society and as fulfilling many of people's affiliation and identity needs. This is reminiscent of Sidel and Sidel's view and highlights also the negative consequences of industrialisation and urbanisation which are somehow believed to be associated with the decline in the extended family. Caution should be exercised in ascribing to self-help the power to articulate a broad-based challenge to these pervasive features of society, since 'self-help can equally be seen as a haphazard, pragmatic response to increasingly evident gaps in statutory services' (Unell, 1987, p. 63).

Yet we can see self-help as a broad-based social movement both in Britain and the US, which has roots in the mainstream of pragmatic thinking. Self-help thus illustrates a particular strain of anti-intellectual thinking, which in Britain is exemplified in a mixture of utilitarian philosophy in the nineteenth century and the current dislike of professionalism embedded in theory, which besets the image of social work practice and training today. Insofar as self-help is still heir to a well-entrenched tradition of amateurism and voluntary effort, links can be made with the British context of mid-Victorian philanthropy in which self-help was first associated, through the Charity Organisation Society, directly with the practice of social work.

Developments in Britain also can be viewed from a critical perspective. Within the domain of professional health and social care, several social and economic factors may have been associated with the growth and spread of self-help. These include the impulse towards decarceration, the contraction of medical and clinical practice and a degree of disillusionment with this, the growth of alternative practice and finally the heightened awareness of consumers of services beyond their situation as more or less stigmatised clients. Further, within social work there has been a tendency since the 1960s for professional power to be viewed more critically, allied with the very distinct but perhaps convergent impulse of social workers towards harnessing the positive influence of networks of consumers of social services in helping activities of many kinds in the community.

How much self-help is there?

This is a very relevant question, given the international character of the field of self-help. The influence of the US on self-help in Western Europe in fact may be no more significant than what has been learned from the developing countries, the illustration of Nijeri Kori in Chapter 4 representing this latter influence. In short, the trans-national nature of self-help cannot be ignored.

The mushrooming literature on self-help in the US, mirrored to a lesser extent in Britain, indicates a high level of interest in both of these countries. But in Britain at any rate, this has not been accompanied by a similar enthusiasm for research (Richardson, 1983, p. 203). Again, some people have suggested that in the US and in Britain self-help is a middle-class phenomenon. Diversification of self-help can be demonstrated through the range of areas covered. Unell charts a variety of group initiatives concerned with different physical conditions and life crises (Unell, 1987, p. 30).

However, there is still little evidence of old people, for instance, taking self-help initiatives. Further, from Unell's admittedly small-scale survey of professionals' views of self-help, it is clear that many see activities as of use to only a limited number of people. There is some truth in the image of self-help groups as catering primarily for middle-class people whose problems do not in any case require professional support or intervention.

In Western Europe, there is evidence of growing interest in self-help. In the Netherlands, there are groups catering for such aspects as euthanasia, suicide, transvestism and sado-masochism (Bakker and Karel, 1983, p. 167). Many of these relate to wider political and social issues and are associated to a degree with increasing awareness of the limitations of statutory health, educa-tion and social welfare provisions. In West Germany, the ecologic-al, peace and women's movements give the impression of much activity in the self-help area. In Belgium, the lack of national funding beyond a few specialist projects contrasts with the growing provincial and local support for self-care and self-help (Branc-kaerts, 1983, p. 158). In France, the strength of private provision alongside public health and social services, and the unpopularity of voluntary action itself, apparently still leaves scope for self-help initiatives either as alternative to, or as compensation for, weak-nesses in the other sectors (Ferrand-Bechmann, 1983, p. 186).

In the developing countries, self-help and mutual aid commonly comprise the core not just of health and social services but also of the economic and social fabric itself. This applies from agriculture to education, from housing to the supply of energy. In most areas, the majority of the people since time immemorial have had to provide their own tools, buildings, skills and other resources, or run the risk of deprivation or death. The problems of Western industrial societies tend to arise from over-production and over-consumption whereas in the Third World the reverse is true.

In the developing countries, self-help by the poor is as much a political issue as anywhere else. For instance, the shift to commun-ity-based, locally non-professionally led campaigns or programmes to change lifestyles, reduce environmental hazards or deal effec-tively with personal health and social problems, may involve confronting exploitive power in societies either apathetic towards, or actively hostile towards any activity implying any change in their policies or practices. In many countries, self-help and self-care are much more of a replacement for non-existent health and social services than complementary with existing provision. Thus, between 65 per cent and 90 per cent of sick people in South and East Asia make use of self-administered herbal remedies (Stokes, 1981, p. 103). Again, research into leprosy in Chad indicates that traditional self-care by lepers is more effective than treatment by the medical services (Stokes, 1981, p. 104).

In writing about social work and self-help in Britain, it is thus as important not to lose sight of the wider international context of the developing countries as it is to take account of developments in Western Europe and the US.

Summary

Chapter 1 has introduced self-help activity insofar as it relates to social work. We have considered the difficulties of defining it, examining examples of the range of its activities and the nature of the values subscribed to by self-helpers. Finally, we have looked at different explanations offered for the popularity of self-help in developed countries in the twentieth century, noting in the process that its incidence is by no means confined to those countries.

2

How Social Workers Relate to Self-Help

Chapter 2 provides a social work context for the more detailed examination of self-help, and sets out three main ways in which social workers relate to self-help activities.

Social work and self-help: a problematic relationship

The fact that social workers have not related as effectively as they might have to the self-help field contrasts with the massive amount of involvement which takes place in related, but quite distinct, areas; for instance, the widespread use of volunteers in social work has been noted (Holme and Maizels, 1978, p. 172). In contrast, six main factors contribute to the relative neglect of self-help by social workers: social trends; constraints on social workers; social workers undervaluing the activities of self-helpers; a lack of confidence about how to proceed; conceptual confusions about professional involvement; a lack of accessible demonstrations of effective practice; and last but not least the underdevelopment of empowerment through self-help.

Social trends affect the focus of activity

The postwar years have seen massive shifts in the resourcing and administering of state provision in social services and consequent redeployments in the balance between statutory, voluntary and private provision. Less dramatically, though no less significantly, arguments in favour of self-help alternatives to social work have been advanced for many years. More than twenty years ago, attention was drawn to the sociological notion of social networks as a non-casework means of supporting the isolated, the elderly and people with handicaps (Goldberg, 1966, p. 73). Administrative structures have certainly changed since that work was written, in a direction which reflects the growing size and strength of the voluntary sector, either independent of, or in partnership with, the statutory sector. The Griffiths Report (Griffiths, 1988, paras 4.3–4, 5, p. 7) notes the importance of the voluntary, private and informal care sectors in providing community care and singles out the voluntary sector in many roles, including that of self-help (Griffiths, 1988, para. 8.11, p. 26).

The current relationship between the fields of social work and self-help practice is influenced by demographic trends, the social, political and economic climate, social policy, organisational changes in social work and social work ideology.

Demographic and economic trends have a tremendous impact on the size and profile of the workloads of social service departments in general and social workers in particular. Rising unemployment, changes in technology and the economic recession in manufacturing have had harsher consequences for the unskilled, semi-skilled and those unable but wanting to retrain, than for the better qualified and the relatively well-off. Conditions of ethnic and cultural diversity in many parts of Britain still leave black people additionally disadvantaged. Women, people with disabilities or in other circumstances attracting social stigma, the young, and inexperienced and older people, are likely to suffer difficulties. People in more than one of the above groups stand a still greater chance of experiencing the inequalities of a divided society.

Increasing life expectancies and a rising divorce rate combine with changing pressures on, and earning and career opportunities for, women in a context where women's expectations are themselves changing. We may be witnessing not so much the decline of the family as a shift towards four-generational systems of caring in households (Wilding, 1986), which produces ever-increasing burdens on a smaller than ever pool of available potential carers. In practical terms, this is the consequence of the demographic trends referred to above. In proportion to the number of dependants, children and old people in particular, the number of able-bodied adults is declining. Within this able-bodied group, the bulk of the task of looking after people in the community falls to female relatives.

Some groups, notably old people and people with disabilities, are particularly vulnerable to poverty, unemployment and a too restricted view of their own rights to qualify for help (Townsend, 1979). The workload of social workers has been affected also by the development of community care policies in work with elderly people, people with disabilities, people with mental illnesses and children and young people. The growing size of the elderly population, in absolute as well as relative terms, leads them to figure prominently as a client group. The increasing trends towards closing down large mental hospitals, hospitals for those with mental handicaps and community homes with education on the premises lead to questions being raised (Audit Commission, 1986) about whether adequate community-based services have been generated to replace them. At the same time, though, we are witnessing the end of the virtual monopoly of social services departments over the provision of residential and day care services in these sectors. Private residential provision, registered but not necessarily quality-controlled by social services departments, has been encouraged in its growth by the willingness of the DHSS to provide funding for residents. Clearly, the state response to people in need is being restructured under the feet of social workers.

The constraints on social workers affect the way they relate to self-help

Far from Seebohm heralding the end of the problems of organising social work, the professional autonomy of social workers continues to be compromised by their accountability to office managers who are distinct from client-contact and motivated by bureaucratic rather than professional imperatives (Toren, 1972). Three trends in social work organisation have been identified: towards greater accountability, towards increasing decentralisation of government and localised delivery of services and towards contracting resources in real terms in relation to the tasks facing professional workers (Boateng, 1986, p. 3). In the face of these somewhat contradictory trends, the administration of social services departments often reinforces accountability to the director rather than to the consumer (Satyamurti, 1981). Social workers are often left to manage as best they can the inevitable tension between their statutory duty to supervise, inspect, to make independent recommendations or decisions and their feeling that they should be creatively challenging the direction of social policies so as to serve the interests of clients, fight for more resources and for freedom to innovate. Rolf Olsen put his finger on these trends in 1982:

> In spite of the growth in services these tasks are often carried out with inadequate resources, an uncertain knowledge base, and as yet unresolved difficulties associated with the reorganisation of the personal social services in 1970. In recent years these difficulties have been compounded by a level of criticism unprecedented since the Poor Law (Foreword to Bamford, 1982).

Social workers are as much gatekeepers of access to resources of support and help as they ever were. There is a necessity for them to work within the compass of an ever-increasing and ever more complex legislative framework of statutory duties, combined with their growing role as child protection officers in the wake of the contemporary wave of child abuse disclosures. This has the effect of edging their other work to the sidelines. Increasingly in areas outside child care, social workers are thus under pressure as enablers of voluntary activity, self-help and self-care.

The activities of self-helpers are undervalued by some professionals

Social workers may claim that they are too busy to devise ways of working with self-helpers, that they have too little resources, that they are too preoccupied with 'essential' tasks. This may not be an intentional snub of the self-help sector, but an underdeveloped relationship with it often can be experienced as undervaluing self-helpers themselves. Research shows that education and training courses for professional social workers tend virtually to ignore the existence and potential of the entire voluntary sector. (Gill and Andrews, 1987). The same is true for self-help. The question is, given the social and political trends, the resource constraints, the pressure on practice, how far can self-help contribute to giving consumers a better social work service and avoid becoming part of a cost-cutting confidence trick played on gullible practitioners and vulnerable consumers?

Conceptual confusion inhibits social work involvement in self-help

Social workers shy away from self-help partly because the interests of self-helpers and social workers sometimes coincide, sometimes overlap and sometimes are distinct or even mutually conflicting. There are contradictions too which arise from these complex relationships. Surely if social care involves negotiating and bringing helping resources to bear on a problem, then it rules out self-help? Surely, the notion of self-help makes the word 'client' inappropriate?

How does a social worker get into the practice of self-help? Perhaps it is no fault of social workers that there is a lack of guidance on how to relate to the field of self-help. But the fact remains that few have developed networks which take them far into the self-help field. Far too often, self-help is seen as marginal to social work, whereas in fact instances can be found in the heartland of its territory. For instance, the principles of self-help sustain the social work which accompanies self-help groups with survivors of sexual abuse (Chapter 3).

Mutual aid and self-help may be assumed to be integral to the development of social care, without any further explanation of the notion of social care itself seeming to be necessary. This is the way in which Richardson and Goodman (1983, p. 1) begin their book on self-help. But social care is not an homogeneous unitary concept. As many as five closely linked kinds of social care have been identified (Payne, 1986, p. 3), in an examination of social work practice which confirms that the idea of social care needs unpacking if it is to help us to be more specific about how social workers relate to the self-help field.

In the sense that social care is concerned with negotiating and enabling more resources to be brought to bear on the helping of clients, strengthening networks of support and extending preventive work, it lends itself to encouraging the development of self-help activities. Clearly, self-help groups are one of the most obvious ways in which resources for the support of social work clients may be mobilised. Social workers may be involved in initiating a group or revitalising or encouraging an existing one.

They may suggest to a client that a particular advice service or community group may be able to help.

In many ways, the Barclay Report (1982) exemplifies the growing tendency for dialogue – not to say overlap – between social work and self-help to be made explicit. In Barclay, social work in general is described as a continuum of activities ranging from professionalised work to the helping carried out by relatives or neighbours (Barclay, 1982, p. xvi). Within this range, the definition of responsibilities and activities of professionally qualified social workers necessitates a more restricted view of what Barclay calls 'formal' social work, embracing the two components of counselling and social care planning (Barclay, 1982, p. xvii). Counselling includes social casework, or direct work with clients through which they are 'helped to change, or to tolerate, some aspects of themselves or their environment' Barclay, 1982, p. xiv). Social care planning covers a variety of activities designed to strengthen the networks, formal and informal, of helping and supportive people, agencies, organisations and services, which may contribute to the response to a client's problems.

Barclay describes the community approach as one of the three approaches to social policy which provide the context for social work. The other two, incidentally, are termed the safety net and welfare state approaches, both of which are variants of the provision of services, giving the voluntary sector a significant and a minor role respectively. In the community approach, however, the voluntary and informal sectors play such a prominent part that state provision becomes more peripheral.

In theory, the community approach has at its core the question of how consumer participation in the delivery of social services can be maximised. Now in a sense, trends in the past twenty years in Britain towards more centralised and bureaucratised social services have been countered by a move towards decentralisation and community involvement (Hadley and McGrath, 1980, p. 7) which converges on the community approach described in the Barclay Report. The advocates of a more full-blooded strategy of decentralisation argue that to be more than tokenistic it needs to be implemented in the context of a belief in the equal merits of voluntary and informal, as against statutory, approaches to social services provision (Hadley and McGrath, 1980, p. 10). The rhetoric of decentralised or community social work all too often contradicts the reality of the low commitment by social services departments to training, supporting, resourcing and empowering volunteers, informal carers and self-helpers.

But the most telling evidence of the problematic status of self-help and empowerment in relation to social work practice comes not from Barclay but from the Statement of Requirements for Qualification in Social Work, passed by CCETSW at its Council meeting of 13 April 1989. There are no direct references to self-help and social work in this, and even the references to empowerment in earlier drafts (See Fifth Draft, Sections 1.4 and 4.3, CCETSW February 1989) have been deleted.

Illustrations of proven effective practice are all too few

This statement applies to the self-help field as much as it does to the larger canvas of the Barclay Report. The attainability of the aims of Barclay are called into question by the lack of readily available illustrations of effective practice to guide their implementation. Critics of Barclay argue that the report is too optimistic about the equating of family care and the voluntary sector with community care. It presents alternative perspectives but not a clear enough fully-costed manifesto advocating one of them and fails in consequence to indicate the need to prioritise the allocation of scarce resources. The report also fails to confront the issue of the distribution of power in social services, with particular regard to the respective situations of the professional and the consumer and does not spell out how community social work could be implemented. Research into attempts to implement seven approaches to community or patch-based social work suggests that they are dogged by three main problems: bureaucracy which works against local autonomy, views of professionalism which emphasise traditional approaches based on individual casework rather than more flexible and open-ended approaches and, finally, trade unionism which may restrict innovation through requiring detailed negotiations between management and unions before change can proceed (Hadley and McGrath, 1980, pp. 101–3). Even by its enthusiasts, the successful implementation of patch-based social services is said to depend on the commitment of managers and other staff, a significant allocation of training resources and the advice of an independent consultant (Hadley *et al.*, 1984, pp. 151–2).

One view of an alternative organisation for social services is provided by Hadley and Hatch (1981, p. 166), involving four principles: plural provision – a variety of community-based voluntary and informal as well as statutory services; decentralisation – the dominance of community-oriented provision; contractual and not hierarchical accountability; participation involving users and providers alongside each other in running local services.

Evidence of the lack of meaningful participation by lay people in the planning and delivery of social services can be gathered from a variety of sources (Beresford and Croft, 1981). Critics of patch schemes of social services provision argue that the advertised advantages such as increased mutual aid and self-help, public participation, democratisation and autonomy of local services, underplay shortcomings in its implementation (Beresford, undated). These criticisms raise questions about the involvement of the voluntary and informal sectors. This is ironic since decentralisation may accompany a tendency towards centralisation and actually shifting power up the hierarchy, token rather than real local democracy and power-sharing and cost-cutting statutory services as self-help develops, rather than extending a partnership between statutory, voluntary and informal provision (Beresford, undated).

One answer to the question as to how social workers can become more confidently involved in self-help is to seek good illustrations of effective practice to see what can be learned from them. One effective way to tackle the above problems is to distinguish between *different forms of relationship* between social work and self-help and then systematically to assess the relevance of each for practice, as we do below.

Empowerment through self-help is under-developed

Although, as we indicated in Chapter 1, the notion of empowerment has emerged in the past few years as a fashionable term to brandish around in social work conferences, we have seen above that its currency is not yet explicitly recognised by CCETSW. Further, it is probably true to say that in Britain at any rate, its application in practice is relatively limited. In fact, there is a lack of readily identifiable guidelines for practitioners and a tendency, as a result, for the term 'empowerment' to be used in a rather loose way. One danger of this is that its significance becomes lessened as its meaning is diluted. Empowerment may thus be used to mean simply 'enablement'. The accounts given of the 1989 BASW conference on empowerment (*Social Work Today*, 13 April 1989, p. 6) confirm the need for the development of more coherent and positive strategies for empowering workers and self-helpers. Whilst the presentation of a comprehensive examination of empowerment is outside the scope of this book. The framework which follows is intended to further the development of empowerment in relation to self-help and social work.

Social work and self-help: a proposed framework

Table 2.1 shows how three types of relationship between social work and self-help may be distinguished from each other, in terms of the degree of resourcing, leadership and support which comes from the professional organisation (which we are assuming here is normally a social work organisation) and the nature of the relationship between the professional and the self-help activity.

Table 2.1   *Relationship between social work and self-help activity*

Characteristic category of self-help	Resourcing by organisation	Leadership by professional	Support by professional	Example of how professional relates to self-help
INTEGRAL	Much or all	Direct	Regular	Innovates and makes activity available as part of service
FACILITATED	Some	Indirect	Intermittent	Stimulates activity
AUTONOMOUS	None	None	None	Refers people to and imports learning from existing activity

Using the analogy of driving, in the case of integral self-help professional social workers are in the driving seat, in the facilitated situation the worker accompanies the hiring self-helper who takes the wheel, whilst in autonomous self-help the self-helper owns the car and drives it independently of professional help.

Integral self-help

It will be evident from Table 2.1 that this is the most paradoxical type of relationship, since self-help activities are apparently rooted in the social work agency and yet apparently exemplify the purposes and goals of self-help. This relationship involves activity promoted, supported and directly led by professionals in a social work organisation which largely or wholly sponsors the self-help. Gartner and Riessman (1977, p. 71) comment that the major health organisations are now sponsoring self-help clubs (for example, the American Cancer Society supports the laryngectomy, mastectomy and ostomy groups and at a recent convention the American Heart Association recommended that its state affiliates encourage and promote the establishment of stroke clubs).

At first sight it looks as though integral self-help is a simple contradiction in terms. But as we shall see in Chapter 3, it provides an attractive option for social workers and self-helpers in some circumstances.

Examples of integral self-help include settings such as the independence unit in the social work facility, often using the words 'self-help' in its title, in which residents or clients involved in day-care are responsible for programming their own activities. They also include self-help groups organised and resourced entirely within a social work agency, but nevertheless run on self-help lines.

Facilitated self-help

This type of relationship occurs where social workers take enabling and indirect action to bring people together or create a climate for activity in some other way. It involves activity in which professionals provide some support and a degree of indirect leadership. Examples of such work come especially from areas of social work such as mental health, where a degree of professional knowledge, skill or resources at the preparatory or early stages of self-help can make the crucial difference between the survival or non-survival of an activity. It has thus been observed that people experiencing depression often find it hard to take the plunge and initiate a self-help group without some professional input in the form of knowledge, skills and resources (Lindenfield and Adams, 1984).

Autonomous self-help

Clearly, the distance between the social worker and self-help can
be seen most clearly in this type of relationship. Yet, in some
senses, this sharpens the need for some articulation of that
relationship itself. This form of self-help is initiated, organised,
resourced and run entirely independently of professionals. Again,
as in the case of integral self-help, it seems at first glance as though
this category of self-help has nothing to do with social work
practice. But as we shall see, because of their subject matter, the
issues they raise, as well as how their connections with social work
are made, autonomous self-help activities deserve particular attention.

Autonomous self-help includes the 'anonymous groups', groups
for people experiencing some form of stigma such as AIDS
sufferers, groups in mental handicap, mental health survivors'
groups, gender-based and consciousness-raising groups.

The structure of Chapters 3–9

Chapters 3–5 describe in turn the three major ways in which social
workers need to tackle the task of relating effectively to self-help.
Chapters 6–9 are concerned with issues which are central to
effective social work practice.

Summary

Chapter 2 has set out the major contemporary factors which
converge to enhance the significance of self-help for social workers, whilst at the same time generating a framework which enables
us to examine how social workers may develop, use and relate to
self-help in different ways, in a variety of settings.

3

How Social Workers May Develop Integral Self-Help

Nature of integral self-help

As we saw in Chapter 2, to all intents and purposes integral self-help is part of the service provided by the social work organisation. It follows that professionals have a direct role to play in ensuring an adequate level of resourcing and support. The factors which affect the degree to which a given activity is considered to be integral include the nature of its focus and the level of professional support. Integral self-help is thus initiated and implemented as part of a social work provision, facility or programme. Inherent in this statement is the paradox of self-help as something provided, but this should not prevent an appreciation of its constructive aspects. It is inescapable that a good deal of self-help in fact is fully-funded and supported by social work organisations. In Chapter 3, we shall examine the implications of this for social workers in their practice.

Criteria influencing the decision to develop integral self-help

In what circumstances is integral self-help the preferred approach? To help us to determine this, two considerations must be balanced against each other: the requirement to protect, support or meet the special needs of the client and the need to respect the rights of the client. Further, there is a need to consider the extent to which the social worker wishes to shift the activity towards facilitated or even autonomous self-help. But the over-riding consideration is the requirement that the worker takes the initiative because of the lack of knowledge, skills or resources of the potential self-helper. This has four aspects:

Without social worker taking the initiative needs would remain unmet

This criterion can also be viewed as the general rationale governing the development of integral self-help. It can be justified in circumstances where potential self-helpers themselves are clearly not in a position to start up a self-help activity. The following criteria help to distinguish these circumstances in which the social worker becomes *proactive* from those discussed in Chapters 4 and 5 where she or he is more or less *reactive*.

Requirement to protect, support or meet special needs

There are circumstances in which this is an over-riding consideration. Social work involvement may be a statutory duty. The assessment of the case may be that the risk of harm to the client or to others will be increased to an unacceptable level if social work involvement in the activity is not maintained.

Requirement to maximise people's involvement in the helping process

Integral self-help is envisaged in situations where clients will benefit from positive participation in helping themselves. This parallels the necessity in all social work for the social worker to bear in mind constantly the rights of the client, including the right to appropriate levels of choice, autonomy and self-determination in the way professionals are involved in her or his life.

Working towards facilitated or autonomous self-help where appropriate

As a general rule, it is likely that the social worker will work towards facilitation and/or autonomy unless in the first or second criteria mentioned above there is a specific reason for not doing so. This is consistent with the general principles of empowerment, discussed further towards the end of this chapter.

Two forms of integral self-help

As far as social workers are concerned, the major difference is between establishing an activity on the assumption that it will remain integral, and developing it with the aim of moving the activity itself towards greater independence and autonomy. We shall look at these in turn.

Permanent: building self-help into social work provision

The emphasis of integral activity is on self-help as part of social work provision. It follows that we need to examine ways of building-in self-help to social work services. The rationale for developing integral self-help is similar to that for social work itself, namely that some people cannot cope without professional help or support in one form or another but that it needs to be provided in such a way as to minimise their dependence and maximise the quality of their lives.

Typically, this form of self-help is open-ended. This has advantages and disadvantages. On one hand, it enables people to move through the activity at their own pace. On the other hand, it entails the risk of fostering dependence not just on the activity but also on the professional.

Specialised self-help units   The justification for a self-help unit will generally be that the unit needs to be permanent, to enable the people using it to move from a situation of lesser to greater independence of professional social work support. The risk is that self-help, which is oriented towards maximising the independence of clients, may actually enable them to be more effectively controlled.

facilities which in other respects might have been viewed in the past as contradicting self-help. Thus, a home for the elderly may have a unit attached which is concerned with promoting independence on the part of some residents. A common rationale for such development may be the desire of some professionals to counteract what they see as harmful effects of institutional living. However, others would argue that there is a place for self-help as part of the normal continuum of social services support. In other words, self-help, self-care and mutual aid should be normal built-in features of residential, day and fieldwork provision.

Groups for people with specialised needs   Another example of this approach is becoming increasingly common, and that is the intensive self-help group set up by one or more social workers for people who need particular support and/or help, perhaps while other work is done with them.

The social work team working with child sexual abuse may be concerned to provide an opportunity for people coming into the agency to have the opportunity to meet and share experiences with each other, where this is appropriate. More than this, they may decide to provide a self-help group for survivors of sexual abuse.

The survivors' groups run in the Glasgow area by the Royal Scottish Society for the Prevention of Cruelty to Children (RSSPCC) illustrate integral self-help. Fundamentally, such groups are informed by the principle that people who have been abused may be in a good position to help others in the same situation, or a similar situation to themselves. Workers who are involved in such initiatives often have experience of setting up and running other self-help groups. Two painful themes converge in such initiatives in the field of physical and sexual abuse. First, the experiences of members of survivors' groups often are so painful that a group needs locating somewhere sufficiently safe to enable the experience of those who stand directly outside the pain of the experience to be drawn on. Second, in contrast, the experiences of members may be so painful that a survivors' group needs to be facilitated by someone who has some direct personal experience with which to be able to help others cope with their anger subsequent to being abused. RSSPCC social workers refer to the difficulties and eventual failure of a group which lacked the involvement of a professional. At the same time, these workers acknowledge that in such circumstances professional social workers may be viewed by women in particular as another imposed power structure, superimposed on the power exercised by the abuser.

The RSSPCC groups tend to be underpinned by a twofold structure of individual counselling for all members without exception and the attendance of two social workers at each group meeting. The counselling by a social worker is a prerequisite for every member before she or he joins a group. It does not stop once attendance at meetings starts but continues in parallel with group sessions. The presence of two social workers at each meeting is held to have several advantages. It provides peer professional support and consultation for each in a context where the proceedings of all meetings are treated as totally confidential. It enables them to be of more use to other group members in a context where meetings often deal with very difficult and emotional subject matter, such as broaches on basic concerns of sexuality. It enables workers to share the task of remaining alert to group processes.

Each group is advertised by social workers to their clients and is open to all save those who are members of other groups, external to the agency. It is necessary to approach people very carefully when inviting them so that they feel perfectly free to refuse.

It has been found that problems can arise when members actively participate simultaneously in more than one group. Experience suggests that whilst in theory there may be no reason to restrict the age of members, in practice there may be problems of compatibility if, for instance, teenagers are present alongside middle-aged people. Further, the experiences of members, such as previous group membership, may cause them to behave with such confidence as to intimidate others. In summary, there is a need to match the pace of the group to the experiences and capacities of members, but in practice a number of factors – not least the subject matter of group activities – will make this difficult. Over and above the survivor's groups, the pattern of integral self-help in the RSSPCC extends to arrangements made by social workers for one victim to meet another in situations where it is felt that mutual help may be given.

Not only do such groups enable people to write about their experiences. Some members may feel that it is only through writing things down that they are able to express them and make it possible to manage their feelings. Some members have undertaken courses of various kinds. In other cases, former victims of abuse have trained and gone on to practise as social workers. It is thus difficult to define the nature of survivors' groups. They are partly therapeutic and partly consciousness-raising and indeed the tension between these elements may be difficult to manage. Further, members of some groups do not like to see the two elements mixing: some feminists, for instance, may see therapy as colonisation by professionals.

In a similar group which arose from the experience of social workers involved in the Cheshire Sexual Abuse Support Line, it was found that childminding and transport to and from the group were invaluable to the meetings, which took place in an anonymous house owned by the social services department (Wilson, 1989, p. 12).

The justification for integral self-help groups in terms of the extent of members' difficulties, makes it highly desirable, if not essential, for more than one social worker to be involved. This makes it possible for co-support, consultation and co-supervision to occur. It also makes it easier for different tasks to be carried out as the group develops. In the Cheshire project, the social workers shifted from providing counselling support to giving practical help and advice and also liaising with others outside the group (Wilson, 1989, p. 13).

Transitional: working towards facilitated or autonomous activity

Whilst integral self-help sometimes involves movement along the continuum towards facilitated or even autonomous activity, this does not necessarily happen, and neither is it always desirable: there may be factors operating which necessitate some consumers of social services continuing to receive high intensity support. Integral self-help is the preferred option where there are specific factors which make it unlikely or undesirable for consumers of social work services to take initiatives and help themselves directly.

The aim of working towards facilitated self-help is inherent in some integral activity from the outset. In such circumstances, it is preferable to make this goal explicit at the start. It may be appropriate to aim for autonomy from professionals such as social workers, in which case this too should be made clear.

The term 'empowerment' is used increasingly in a range of settings and with many different nuances of meaning, sometimes to facilitate efforts to develop integral self-help which moves towards facilitated or autonomous self-help. In this section, attention is given to the general principles of this approach to self-help, rather than to spelling out what empowerment means in all its forms.

Empowerment and self-help: a problematic process   Empowerment is becoming the 'buzz word' of the late 1980s. It can be

defined as the process by which individuals, groups and/or communities become able to take control of their circumstances and
achieve their own goals, thereby being able to work towards
maximising the quality of their lives. The process of empowerment
operates at the levels of the individual, group, family, organisation
and community, and also in the different sectors of people's lives.
One person may feel empowered because of something realised or
understood, another may experience empowerment once a new
job, course or career opportunity is achieved.

By the nature of the popularity of the concept of empowerment,
there is a danger of attaching it to social work activities in an
inappropriate way and also of reducing its scope and also its power
to improve people's circumstances. For instance, the cutting edge
of the concept of empowerment is blunted by the tendency to
speak as though it is merely another form of *enabling* act by
professionals. Empowerment may also be applied not only to
clients as self-helpers but also to social workers themselves. Whilst
valid, this deflects attention away from the clients who should be
the main focus of empowerment activities.

An example of an attempt to empower people is provided by the
Humberside Project, a partnership between Save the Children
Fund and Humberside Social Services Department. This aims to
create a series of self-help neighbourhood settings and leading to
shared management of resources devoted to work with parents
and children. Initially, the emphasis has been on the under-fives
and the first two work bases have included a council house and an
existing playgroup on two housing estates in Grimsby. Project staff
aim throughout to encourage parents to take a lead in making
decisions about the kinds of activities and provision for young
children they would like in the neighbourhood. Since December
1986 when project workers started, parents have become involved
in running drop-in facilities for parents and toddlers and play-
groups elsewhere on the estates, as well as groups exclusively for
mothers.

The concept of user involvement in management is central to
the Humberside Project. It was nurtured through three years of
planning before implementation, during which staff in Save the
Children Fund (SCF) and Humberside Social Services worked
through issues concerning partnership. Eventually it was agreed
that during the developmental period the project would be run by

SCF, serviced by their regional resources and development worker, other staff salaries and expenses being met by social services in anticipation of the eventual handover of the entire project to the social services department, some five years after its commencement.

It is too early to assess the degree to which the handover of management of the project to local users, as originally envisaged by the agencies, has been achieved, but less than a year after the commencement of work at the first workbase, workers and parents were agreed that progress had been made. An evaluation of this project carried out by the writer produced the following illustration of the empowerment process, from the perception of a neighbourhood team manager, responsible for the range of social services in one of the estates served by the project:

> You obviously want a small unit of the kind we envisaged: a continual throughput, people come, they make contact, they grow, they develop, they get confidence, they move out and start to do likewise elsewhere . . . We are significantly down the road towards local management, local people using the project. I had anticipated a build-up of local people, wanting to be involved in decision-making. In fact the pressure from them is quite strong, wanting to be involved in things . . . The ripples are going outward now, wider, to more organisations now, and I hope going out to a higher range as well, so that it's more an assumed attitude people have towards their children and their needs rather than just a build-up of social facilities or a collection of activities. It's much more comprehensive than that . . . the local authority almost becomes a local financial source only and people locally feel themselves sufficiently confident in handling their own affairs to run something which operates reasonably cheaply and provides a service which keys together everything that's going on in the neighbourhood.

Integral self-help involves the paradox that sponsoring social work agencies resource and professionally support the move towards self-help by consumers of their services. The manager quoted above describes this:

> You do have to keep some kind of hand on the tiller, you do have to think about it as an organisation and give it the kind of support and developmental help that it needs from time to time. But I see it ultimately very much as an enabling function community work-wise, which sustains the growth and developmental of something which is very much about empowering local people.

Associated with the empowerment process, it is typical to encounter a variety of resources being brought to bear, some of which lie outside the range of social work provision. In this respect, the social worker acts as the negotiator who initiates the activity and then builds up a multi-disciplinary, multi-professional approach. Thus, in the Humberside Project, from the initial overtures made to parents a number of training courses developed, in aspects of play and parenting. At a later stage, parents undertook courses together, arranged on-site, which led to a number becoming registered as play leaders. From that point, they were able to share with project workers, as volunteers and as paid workers themselves, some of the basic tasks of supervising play activities and ensure that there was time and resources to carry out further development work in the community.

Several themes emerge from such projects, which have more general relevance to the empowerment endeavours of social workers:

The paradox of power   The concept of empowerment through integral self-help implies the paradox that professionals exercise power in their commitment to providing the initial resources and the stimulus of suggesting directions in which the activities move, but at the same time try to stand back and let the self-helpers put their own definition on what happens.

Whose definition of the goals of empowerment do we accept?   The very fashionability of empowerment as a goal of workers involved in developing self-help heightens a dilemma for practice: whether to proceed on the basis of the view of the social worker or of the potential self-helpers. It is common to find parents involved in the early stages of such initiatives as the Humberside Project expressing hesitance about, or even refusing to consider, taking on responsibility for managing the project. Should the workers proceed with goals they themselves have determined, or accept from the outset a view of the activity as defined by the parents themselves? This is a difficult question, to which there is no easy answer. In many ways, the most realistic approach is to maintain open dialogue between social workers and self-helpers about such issues from the earliest days. There is some evidence that as the latter develop in confidence and competence, their ambitions to take on a more participative role in the activity also grow.

Personal growth and professional competence   It is important to develop a view of empowerment through self-help which recognises these two as linked themes for both social workers and self-helpers, rather than as separated by the roles of professional and user. Ideally, empowerment as a process should embrace all parties to social work: workers, clients, organisations, self-helpers and all networks.

An open-ended process rather than single-outcome activity   The most noticeable feature of this approach to self-help is the lack of one single milestone which could be said to mark the outcome of the project. Instead, typically activities are perceived as processes, in which the personal and professional aspects referred to above develop in an open-ended way. One of the striking features of such processes is the way professional and self-helper exchange roles and responsibilities as the project moves on. Thus, in the Humberside Project, quite quickly one of the parents, a mother who had never taken this kind of task on before, used the support of the project to start two new parent and toddler groups. She commented that 'Instead of being just a housewife I am beginning to feel important especially when the mums at the group come to me for help and advice. I feel that I am a seed from the project that has grown and is now planting her own seeds'.

A replicable approach   In answer to queries about whether the above activity is central to the social work task, two comments are necessary: first, it is increasingly common to find health, education, social work and voluntary agencies combining with parents in self-help groups, to develop better facilities for parents and children under five; second, this example provides a model which is easily transferable to other client groups in different geographical locations.

Towards community education   In setting out the agenda of empowerment in this section, partly in terms of the goal of shifting from integral to autonomous self-help, we need to make explicit the continuum which exists between what social workers engage in and the work of community educators. In the Humberside Project, one of the most exciting developments has been the establishing by the project workers of a new series of basic courses in family and neighbourhood work, in conjunction with local adult education staff in Grimsby. Undoubtedly, there is much scope for social workers to work across professional boundaries with educational providers and improve both access and ladders of opportunity and qualification in many sectors of learning. Community education is not just new classes in the community. It should be voluntarily negotiated, community-derived learning, which non-professionals can initiate as a means of reducing social inequalities, promoting change and empowering people.

While all this is going on, the paradox of integral self-help is that even if the transitional form is adopted, and progress is made towards people taking over, this is in the context of overall guidance of the processes to which we have made reference, by the professional social worker.

Practice issues

We conclude this chapter by noting some of the main general issues which may arise and need to be taken into account, in the practice of integral self-help.

Clarity about conditions for effective integral self-help

The professional should appreciate at the outset the conditions which influence the choice of this approach to self-help. An early task is to assess the situation. The key factors which determine an integral approach arise from the nature of relevant agencies delivering social work services and the situations of consumers in respect of their problems and the availability of resources to deal with them.

The identity of activity in legal terms should be selected and specified with care. Legal and policy obstacles need to be mini-mised. Effective developments are predicated on effective means by which issues arising can be tackled quickly and effectively. Partnerships between statutory and voluntary organisations are becoming more common and in such cases the existence of adequate collaborative mechanisms is even more important. An adequate organisational base should be identified, with attention to a degree of neutrality in terms of physical location and agency support which guarantees the integrity of the self-help activities. Efforts should be made to identify sources of necessary resources, and if possible to guarantee them, before the activity is initiated. A successful pilot venture funded from another source may suffice to persuade potential resourcers to support the venture.

The specification of focus of the activity should be done with care, in order to minimise the risk of likelihood of failure through dilution of effort or lack of clarity about what is being undertaken. Throughout, social workers as professionals should appreciate that the paradox of empowerment as integral self-help is that it involves giving people back power, rather than acknowledging that people have it and merely enabling them.

Recognition of self-help as a personal and a collective process

Self-help is concerned with the personal growth and development of the individual as well as with the way groups of people engage collectively in self-help activities. It is mistaken, and may be totally stultifying, to see the development of integral self-help, or even self-helping itself, as one process, or as something in which individuals engage, apart from others. The process of self-help itself involves the definition of the process, a paradox which may repeat itself many times as the activity changes, develops or fades out.

Maximal participation of self-helpers throughout the process

All too often, schemes and projects are conjured up by professionals, money is found, staff time is allocated, proposals are worked out in detail, before anyone thinks of consulting the people who are meant to be central – the self-helpers themselves. The rhetoric of the development of empowerment through self-help needs to be reflected throughout the reality of the process of empowering people.

There is thus a need to avoid professionals dictating the agenda of activity, and this implies living with the risk of a lack of consumer leadership by self-helpers. Inherently, social workers occupy strategic positions in relation both to their legal obligations and to their organisational base. The implementation of self-help necessitates a careful handling of the process of development itself. It is all to easy for professionals to misuse their undoubted structural power and damage initiatives, possibly irretrievably.

Acceptance that self-help is chosen and paced by the self-helper

Central to the process is the principle that the social worker as the professional does not impose the process of self-help on a person. Individuals may be given the option of taking part. Once involved, they should have control over the process: the pace of the activity should be determined by the self-helper and not by the social worker.

Setting a long enough time scale

It is important to recognise that the process of shifting from integral to autonomous activity takes time. In the US, where empowerment-oriented self-help programmes have been running for many years, a Director of SCF has described to the writer the typical time scale for this process as ten to twelve years.

The development of integral self-help is slow. There is a need to develop a network of contacts in an area, overcome people's lack of willingness to confide in officials, build up trust and avoid being matronising or patronising towards people. Individuals or groups such as carers' groups seeking advice or information may prefer to get support from a professional, rather than to seek it from a friend or neighbour who then would know things about them they would rather keep private.

Professionals should help their agencies learn from experience

To the extent that the development of a self-help project leads to novel and perhaps instructive ways of approaching a task or service, there should be ways of feeding in this experience constructively to the social work agency itself. For example, in the Humberside Project, management in both voluntary agency and social services could have examined usefully the learning derived in the project from staff working as a 'flat team' without a recognised project leader. How would such experience translate, for example, into the running of a day centre or a residential home?

Summary

In Chapter 3, we have surveyed integral self-help – that is, self-help as part of the services of a social work organisation. The illustrations given have enabled us to make a number of observations on the factors which encourage effective integral self-help.

4

How to Facilitate Self-Help

Nature of facilitated self-help

By definition, facilitation implies a degree of social work involvement. Facilitated self-help involves social workers taking action to bring people together in the first instance and supporting them subsequently in self-help. In the related but distinct context of her study of the Nottingham Self-Help Project, Judith Unell identifies six elements which are inherent in support of self-help: the direct provision of practical resources, the provision of access to practical resources elsewhere, putting people in touch with each other, creating opportunities for different groups to keep in touch and meet, promoting the idea of self-help among professionals and giving new groups specific help (Unell, 1987, pp. 6–7).

In facilitating self-help, the role of the social worker may be summarised as follows:

1. Establishing at the outset a boundary rather than a central role for the social worker
2. Not taking the lead in determining the focus, the pace of activity, the goals or the means of getting there
3. Standing alongside the self-helpers rather than above them in terms of power, skills and professional activity
4. Acting as someone who is available to be consulted rather than as an imposed, supervisory presence.

Criteria affecting appropriateness of facilitated self-help

Two main distinct but to an extent overlapping criteria exist, either of which will suffice to justify a social worker getting involved in facilitating self-help.

1. The expressed wish of potential or actual self-helpers for some advice, help and/or support in setting up and/or maintaining a self-help activity
2. The need as perceived by a social worker for the initiation of a self-help activity, involving self-helpers who have the requisite knowledge, skills and resources to run the activity themselves, given a level of help from the social worker.

Forms of facilitated self-help

The distinction made in Chapter 3 between so-called *permanent* and *transitional* forms of self-help applies here. That is, the activity may be initiated in the expectation that it will continue with the level of social work facilitation significantly unchanged. Alternatively, it may involve a gradual shift towards more autonomous activity, as a consequence of which the social worker will gradually withdraw.

Additionally, we can distinguish between the kind of *direct* facilitation the social worker provides in helping a new activity into being, from the *indirect* facilitation which necessitates the social worker standing outside the activity but providing support and consultation as appropriate.

Permanent facilitated self-help

In the following illustration, before a carefully structured, significant level of support was formulated for groups, they tended to collapse, either because members were demotivated at the outset because of their state of mind, or because they lacked the confidence, skills and/or resources to run the activities effectively.

Mind Your Self is a Leeds-based project founded in the late 1970s and originally sponsored by the Leeds Association for Mental Health. It consists of a network of groups, short course and other associated activities in which non-professional self-helpers have a leading part, the support of a professional social worker, and other workers playing a crucial role. The history of the project illustrates the nature of facilitation by the professional, who began to offer therapeutic support to groups of people with mental health problems in an attempt to counteract the tendency for their groups to be short-lived failures (Adams and Lindenfield, 1985, p. 19). The worker identified with members of groups the following problems they experienced: 'low self-esteem, lack of assertiveness, poor communication skills, lack of spontaneity, lack of physical energy, inability to trust, inability to take risks and no goals or sense of direction' (Adams and Lindenfield, 1985, p. 20). They produced a list of the qualities groups need in order to be effective: even participation, effective leadership, clear goals, good communication, ability to act and flexibility (Adams and Lindenfield, 1985, p. 21). 'As a result of this, we made a bargain. If they agreed to continue meeting weekly on their own, every third week I would work with them on these problems as a therapist. As a result, the group began to flourish. Several very good leaders emerged and began to take responsibility. A new partnership was born in this way, between myself and the group' (Adams and Lindenfield, 1985, p. 21).

In Mind Your Self, it appears that the general lack of problems of members becoming violent or refusing to leave a group, reflects a shared philosophy in groups of a good deal of individual freedom on one hand and a measure of collective responsibility for behaviour on the other. However, it has been noted in Mind Your Self that the need for members involved in leading groups to have some kind of consultancy or supervision from outside the groups is as important for non-professionals as it is for professionals.

Perhaps a pay-off of this form of facilitation is the growth in confidence of self-helpers. Members of Mind Your Self have begun to consider organising short courses on such topics as 'Diet', 'Getting out of a Rut' and 'Middle Age'.

The innovative features of Mind Your Self exemplify the relative willingness of people in the voluntary or self-help sectors to take risks, in contrast with many of their counterparts in statutory social work agencies.

Whilst the strength of this form of facilitation clearly lies in the availability of professional leadership, there is a risk that the social worker will perpetuate this, rather than withdrawing. The problem is how to pace the withdrawal so that self-helpers can feel competent and not experience disablement or the collapse of the activity.

Transitional facilitated self-help

Starting point: identifying the need for action   June is a social worker who has worked in conjunction with a voluntary organisation concerned with mental health and has become aware of the number of phone calls received from people wanting help of various kinds. The difficulty is that callers asking for advice about depression, tranquillisers, phobias and so on invariably do not want to give an address for information to be sent and tend not to ring back for a further chat with a worker. In one or two cases, people have been given information, including invitations to come to chat to a worker.

June talks it over with colleagues in the voluntary organisation and they decide to mobilise a self-help group. Drawing on experience gained from other self-help projects in mental health, they follow a series of stages designed to maximise support to people who may become involved, maximising also the self-help element.

Determining how to respond   June and members of the local voluntary organisation take a number of considered and purposeful decisions based on their estimate of the need which exists and information they collate, which together with their previous experience points towards the potential benefit of facilitating a self-help group. Before acting, they agree on the principles to which they are committed, which will be reflected in any decisions they take subsequently. This is important to them because at this stage they cannot anticipate in detail what might happen, although they have certain expectations.

The decision to facilitate a group follows partly from the picture gained of a typical caller with a problem, who is worried enough to contact the agency but apparently has not the confidence to follow it up. It follows also from experience of one of the workers in the voluntary organisation, who was a member of a self-help group which failed. She shares this experience with June, who correlates it with what she has read.

It appears that half a dozen people who were trying to cope with various mental health problems, the most common being depression, accepted an invitation to meet and talk regularly with each other, but that after a couple of meetings only two were left and then the group collapsed altogether.

June and her colleagues take action to ensure that their facilitated group learns from these experiences. This involves offering to people invited to join a self-help group a clear agreement that a measure of support will be provided at the outset with the *resources* entailed in setting up and maintaining the group, accompanied by specific help with the development of the *skills* members will need to run meetings.

Settling the purpose of the group   The purpose of the group can be defined for its potential members even before it has its first meeting, so as to enable them to manage their own problems. To that end, June ensures right from the start that everyone realises her role is to get the group going. Subsequently, she will withdraw to a position of marginal involvement from which she can service the group if members call upon her.

Planning and programming   The steps June and her colleagues take include finding a suitable room for meetings to take place and ensuring that it is reasonably comfortable and has access to a power point for the making of refreshments. Given the feelings of many callers about their experiences as clients, the decision is taken to use a room in the building housing the local Council of Voluntary Service. Rent will have to be paid from some source if the group continues, but for the initial meetings this and other expenses are met from agency funds. The meeting room thus is on *neutral territory*, which may be crucial to people who have experienced the stigma of being clients or patients.

A number of advertisements are placed in local shop windows and agency offices, inviting people to an initial meeting, also mentioned to callers where appropriate. Articles carefully placed in the columns of local newspapers dealing with voluntary organisations and activities using pen sketches of typical problems prove productive.

At the first meeting, June and her colleague from the voluntary organisation take steps to defuse people's fears as they arrive. Coffee, tea and biscuits are provided and people introduce themselves to each other. A short series of meetings may be planned, after people's expectations and fears have been shared. June makes sure that she offers sufficient support in this process to hold the group together. She anticipates that the needs of the group in its early stages will be for *adequate leadership* and the acquisition of *skills and techniques* to enable its objectives to be determined and worked towards.

Developing rules and procedures   In the early meetings, June and her colleague from the voluntary organisation help the members to draw up a number of *simple rules*. These clarify whether the group is open-ended, how often it will meet, how long each meeting runs, what the pattern of activities is and so on. From experience, she knows that reaching agreement about these can take time.

Of course, there is no reason why a particular structured and formalised system of rules should be worked out. But it often helps to see an example of what somebody else has used in practice, even if this serves only to reinforce one's prior conclusion that it would be better not to set anything up in advance. Justification for the latter is provided by those who prefer to leave it to the group to arrive at its own collective decisions, completely unaided. However, for those who prefer the former approach, an example of the kinds of rules which can operate is provided by Integrity Groups, mentioned in Chapter 1, for which the 15 guidelines paraphrased below provide a helpful basis for working out the kinds of guidelines which may apply in a particular case:

1. Any member threatening or carrying out physical violence against people or things may be summarily expelled
2. Anyone walking out during the process of working through a problem or feeling will be judged to have resigned permanently from the group
3. Anyone can use *any* language or wordless sounds during a group meeting
4. Sub-grouping, that is whispering to one's neighbour, is not allowed
5. Non-attenders should notify the group in advance, giving their reasons
6. Late attenders who do not warn the group in advance may be asked to explain their lateness
7. Discussions between members on group matters between group meetings should be reported at the next group meeting, though such friendships are encouraged

8. Members who tell each other's stories outside group meetings to non-members may be expelled for breaching confidentiality
9. Members are free to leave after three hours of a meeting, even though it has not finished
10. Any member can leave a meeting suddenly, but would be encouraged to talk about it first
11. If the group cannot meet members' needs in normal weekly meetings, then extra meetings may be called
12. If an individual feels he or she is not making progress, or a crisis arises, then an extra meeting may be called by her or him to deal with this
13. The task of chairperson circulates at meetings and should be carried out flexibly and inventively
14. Someone who has a grievance against a different group's member, after discussion in the group, should seek the chance of taking it up with that person in the other group
15. Communities with two or more Integrity Groups may exchange members between groups every few months (Mowrer, 1972, pp. 26–7).

Given this degree of structure combined with the flexibility and open-endedness of possible practices, perhaps it is unsurprising that for many people Integrity Groups can become 'a distinctive sub-culture and way of life' (Mowrer, 1972, p. 26).

Withdrawing as effective leadership emerges   June anticipates that she will be able to withdraw from her direct role and, with her colleague, negotiate that they attend only occasionally, once one or more members have taken over responsibility for running the group effectively.

This is a particularly difficult decision to make and the group may not make it any easier, by finding various ways to indicate how essential the presence of the social worker is to each meeting. In addition, despite the best intentions of the worker, it may be tempting to believe that one is indispensible to the group. However, discussion with group members, colleagues (when they are involved) and honest assessment of one's position will help to clarify the level of participation and support actually needed by the group. There is no reason why the worker should not reach an agreement with other group members about a minimal, though significant, presence which does not intrude too much. For instance, the worker may occupy another part of the building and be technically available for consultation in emergencies. Or, she or he may agree to appear after the meetings have ended for a cup of tea. This is a situation where some imagination needs to be combined with a sensitivity to the needs of group members.

Direct facilitation

In this case, the social worker takes on aspects of the leadership role in the self-help activity. As we shall see, the key to success lies in the balance maintained between initial leading in and subsequent taking a back seat. This is much easier to prescribe than to achieve in practice.

Getting the activity started   The role of the social worker in helping a new project off the ground in a locality involves groundwork of one sort or another, determining the focus, finding the setting, building up the demand for the activity, and then plunging in and arranging the first meeting.

The activity may take place after evidence has been produced of a local need, or partly at the initiative of potential self-helpers themselves, or a combination of these.

Putting people in touch with each other   This is more or less a requirement and may involve setting up a meeting prior to the activity itself. It is possible that any or all of the following four elements may be necessary before the activity itself can be facilitated:

- Creating opportunities for groups to meet
- Doing groundwork with potential self-helpers
- Raising awareness of the issue through publicity: letters to local newspapers, posters, and so on
- Legitimising the self-help activity.

This last point is often missed. The social worker may actually need to overcome ignorance, prejudice or various other resistances to the proposed activity. It may be necessary to convince people of the value of what is intended. In the case of potential self-helpers who are present or recent clients, they may feel it necessary to seek permission, more or less formally, from their workers to take part in the activity. This may involve the social worker in some delicate liaison work, if the confidentiality of the involvement of the individual self-helper needs to be preserved. It is important to recognise the extent to which other social workers and community psychiatric nurses may be viewed as doorkeepers of local resources whose support is necessary before some people can participate in a new activity.

Carrying out initial surveys to establish the extent of need/demand In some ways the social worker functions like a voluntary organisation, aiming to provide a service and in the process a model of good practice. It may be necessary for her or him to justify the proposal to colleagues and to agency managers, in which case a prior survey will have to be carried out, to produce some valid evidence. This is the kind of activity that some workers will be able to delegate to a suitable student, although the amount of supervisory and consultative work is still likely to be considerable.

Obtaining guarantees of adequate resourcing The worker who undertakes the direct facilitation of the activity needs to attend also to the bread-and-butter issues of finding somewhere to meet, ensuring it is adequately heated, making arrangements for a kettle to be available and all the other concerns which arise in Chapter 6.

Of course, these tasks may not be completed prior to the activity being established. There is something to be said for the solidarity and sense of togetherness which grows out of participants taking on these tasks together. The choice of which road depends very much on the focus of the activity and whether the social worker, and other participants, feel there is as much to be gained from the journey as from actually arriving at the destination.

How to proceed: the stepping stones procedure A convenient way to conceptualise the process of direct facilitation by one or more social workers is through the image of 'stepping stones'. The facilitator needs to provide stepping stones for people who have, perhaps, been on the receiving end of professional services which have left them needing to build up self-confidence and independence. For example, in Mind Your Self referred to above, many have been in mental hospitals and have experienced institutionalisation with consequent losses in their ability to make decisions. At the outset the social worker thus takes on much more of the responsibility, only gradually taking a back seat as other participants in the self-help activities begin to follow her or him along the various tasks involving leadership. It is thus convenient to remind self-helpers of the notion of leadership as a multiple series of activities and processes, rather than as all being wrapped up in a single parcel which one person holds.

The relationship between professionals and self-helpers in facilitated situations clearly is complicated by the power imbalance between them. Further, there is no doubt that the leadership role in activities is problematic, especially in the early life of a group. To the extent that participants have experienced being on the receiving end of professional help for a long time, and particularly if they have spent long periods in institutions, they may find it difficult to make the transition to becoming active leaders in a self-help situation.

The fact that Britain is in part heir to a tradition of facilitation of self-help projects inherited from the Third World, invites illustration of a well-established scheme called Nijeri Kori, endeavouring to bring about the establishment of a network of consciousness-raising groups in Bangladesh.

Nijeri Kori means literally 'we do it ourselves', and was started in the late 1970s by a couple of Bangladeshi people concerned to find a more productive approach to development than traditional strategies concerned with agriculture, co-operatives and health care and in which the political dimension was often lacking. Instead, Nijeri Kori now has about 120 staff, based in Dacca, Bangladesh, works in four or five of the poorest parts of the country, and concentrates on consciousness-raising and organising, through demystifying the powerlessness many people feel and giving them back some strength in collective action. Priority is also given to working with women. Workers are drawn from the area, trained and sent back to live alongside the landless and poorest. Over a period of working alongside people, they encourage informal discussion in a group, perhaps using a local event, a tragedy, as a means of bringing people together in mutual solidarity. Subsequently, groups are encouraged to meet for a couple of hours about once a week with the worker and chat about their children, problems of not having enough money, clothes, land, problems of relationship with their husbands. They tend not to call them meetings, but 'sitting together'. Because in that society women traditionally do not speak in mixed groups, women meet separately from men, until they have become confident enough to meet with the men. Later the groups meet without the worker and form a local committee, represented equally by members of women's and men's groups.

The principle involves a lengthy process of talking and thinking and thereby raising the confidence of women in particular to speak out about their situation.

Nijeri Kori is supported partly by War on Want and the following extract is from an account given to the writer for this book by Helen Allison from that organisation. The process of gradually accumulating confidence among women in male-dominated settings is reminiscent of situations in Britain where groups are discriminated against and oppressed. However, the impact of this facilitated self-help group on that situation over a period of time emerges in the account:

'it's quite spectacular to see. In one area we went to we sat in this little bedroom. All the women were there and then as soon as the meeting started and we were introduced all the women left and all the men moved in and sat on the bed. So we said "where are the women? We want to talk to the women". So the message went out that we wanted to see the women. Four women came back in and they sat on the bed. So the men moved over to the side and then gradually over a period of half an hour or an hour more women came in until the room was crowded. And we sat there for about two hours talking to them and the men stayed quiet for that whole period and listened to the women, partly because we were there undoubtedly. But they didn't interrupt, they didn't contradict. Even though initially the women were very shy and hid their faces and giggled and looked embarrassed, they got over that and talked very straightforwardly about simple things like their kids and their money, but also about more complicated things like how they were involved in Nijeri Kori and what the group meant to them, what they see as the possibilities for change and what they would like to see for their kids in the future . . . The only way of bringing about significant change is where people can organise and demand it and it may take a long time but I think in the long run it's more significant than just changing political parties . . . The idea is that once people get more conscious and get more confident and begin to organise locally, that they can then decide for themselves where they want to go, they may decide to join a political party, they may decide to take local action, to make protests against local injustice. There have been cases where people have actually marched on the local government office and demanded certain things. They've also taken up specific cases, like women have protested about wife-beating, which is quite unheard of. If one member of a group has been beaten either by her husband or by her brother-in-law, the women protesting about this would go to the man and try to shame him in public. Meantime, if he was involved in Nijeri Kori then the men's group would also be trying to tackle that issue and discussing it' (interview with Helen Allison, War on Want, 1987).

Indirect facilitation

Circumstances may arise where a social worker is approached or otherwise feels it is appropriate for some self-help venture to be started. In this situation, the provision of information may be sufficient to initiate a project.

So, in the case of indirect facilitation, the help given by the social worker is at one remove from the self-help activity, in the form of consultation or advice, for instance. Indirect facilitation may also take the form of putting people in touch with sources of help and giving information.

Saving money seems to provide a useful focus for many groups, as occurs when a Credit Union is started. With money saved jointly, people who have never owned anything can rent land or buy something essential for the community and collectively manage it. This gives them a sense of power as a group.

A parallel with social work can be drawn in this instance from the field of housing and planning. In recent years a number of projects have arisen as a consequence of the motivation of people to build their own homes. The *self-build* movement as some call it, tussles with the same issues which preoccupy social workers: principally, how to achieve what the self-builders want, without them falling foul of all the legal, building and planning regulations and procedures which normally mean that professional planners and architects take over such schemes. Two authors who have studied this area expound four useful principles governing what they call 'community architecture', which can be applied to self-help and social work:

1. Individuals and families are given the maximum possible control over, and responsibility for, the design and management of their own homes
2. An organisational mechanism is developed for people living in close proximity to communicate with each other and take joint responsibility for common land and facilities
3. Both individuals and communities are able to develop a working relationship with professionals with appropriate technical expertise
4. The partnership of residents and professionals makes it its business to tackle all aspects of the residents' environment, developing both design and organisational solutions simultaneously (Wates and Knevitt, 1987, p. 85).

Corroboration of the benefits of such self-help initiatives in the self-build field has generated a number of indicators of both the potential benefits and limitations of self-help in the area of social work. Consideration by a group of architectural students of fourteen self-build projects in different parts of Britain thus enabled three initial assumptions to be evaluated in the light of experience:

1. That self-build would lead to enhanced community consciousness, heightened trust between people and the sharing of amenities. This tended to happen only in areas where people already knew each other and where self-build effort was only an extension of existing community consciousness
2. That self-build would produce more imaginative responses to problems than traditional approaches

   But while middle-class intellectual groups could do this to a degree, several schemes 'were indistinguishable from the standard mid-income speculative estates, which are found all over Britain'. Further, there was evidence that working-class groups tended to suffer from constraints of needing to seek external finance and their efforts reflected their inability to break away from 'strong overall social pressure and image of the "ideal house" so successfully cultured through advertising' (Arscott, 1976, Section 4)
3. 'That this process of self-build would raise the self-confidence,

awareness and experience of the whole groups, and this in
turn would enable them . . . critically to examine other parts of
their lives. Such a consequence may then, if necessary, lead
the group to seek greater control over the whole of their lives'
(Arscott, 1976, Section 4).

Problems of finance and the lack of innovative motives, purposes
and goals on the part of the self-builders meant that often
self-build merely enabled people to substitute sweat for capital and
painfully achieve their aim of a house on the cheap. Additionally,
'although motivation may be a very important reason for the
outcome, even the more ideologically motivated groups found
barriers and difficulties which are not easily overcome' (Arscott,
1976, Section 4).

From these observations we can draw some parallels with social
work, with particular regard to the need for caution and modest
expectations of self-help at the community level (Woolley, 1985).
Also, as Tom Woolley observed to the writer, the capacity of this
approach to induce change is limited not just by external factors
but also by the need to free self-helpers from parasitic professionals. The initial motivation of participants, their purposes, their
social class and access to resources are all factors which can free
them from some of the burdens of innovating in a resource-
constrained environment.

Practice issues

Facilitation by social workers needs to be purposeful

There is no doubt that many self-help activities exist which
perform a useful function for their members. However, the
following illustration serves as a caution against involvement in an
existing activity in the absence of adequate information about
what it actually can offer self-helpers and social workers.

A survey of active members of Recovery, a large self-help
organisation in the US, with many affiliated groups, as long as
thirty years ago, found that the typical member was a middle-class,
middle-aged, moderately educated married woman with a husband in non-manual work (Wechsler, 1960, p. 302). Most had not

had extensive histories of hospitalisation, over half had none, and a fifth had had no professional treatment at all before joining Recovery. This coincides with the aim of the organisation's facilitator, to recruit those with relatively mild mental health problems. As many as a third had been members for one to two years and a further third for three years or more, a third of all members saying they no longer needed to attend. This indicates the social function performed for members by many self-help groups. However, it should be borne in mind that the support offered by the organisation may not be available from any other source. In fact, Recovery exemplifies the situation of the well-established self-help group or organisation, which may be looked to by potential members and professionals as capable of dealing with problems at an intensity comparable with established agencies. But in fact organisations like this cannot do so, since members tend not to be screened on entry, neither are leaders sufficiently selected, trained or professionally supported to guarantee this.

Minimising the risk of professional colonisation

There is a risk that professionals will take over activities and co-opt self-helpers (see Chapter 8). In the process, professionals may exploit self-help initiatives while seeming to promote them, keeping themselves at the centre of the stage in the process.

Maintaining a balance between leading and facilitating

It is difficult for social workers to provide just sufficient leadership to enable the self-help activity to develop, yet not so much that self-helpers are swamped.

Ensuring blurring of professional and self-help roles

Undoubtedly there is an ambiguity about the balance of power between professionals and self-helpers in many facilitated situations. But this is no more problematic than the ambiguous situation of many participants themselves. For example, there is no denying that it was hard for Doctor Mowrer, starting his first self-help therapy 'Integrity' Group in a mental hospital, to open with the comment that he too had been a patient in a mental hospital. But this cannot deny the reality of his professional position at the point the group started (Mowrer, 1964, p. 108). Mowrer also expresses more general ambivalence, symptomatic of activity in this field. On one hand, he suggests that in the mental health field the stimulus for self-help comes as strongly as it ever did from the grassroots rather than from professionals (Mowrer, 1984, p. 145). Yet he acknowledges Lieberman and Borman's comment that many groups have had significant professional involvement in their inception and development (Mowrer, 1984, p. 143).

Although social workers may play a part as initiators, once it gets going, the activity remains largely managed and carried out by self-helpers themselves. Social work support is thus likely to be more intermittent and the level of resourcing much less than in situations where self-help is integral. But the central feature of facilitated self-help is the type of enabling leadership provided by the social worker. It should be emphasised that self-help activities which are facilitated in their early stages, later may become autonomous as participants acquire the necessary resources, skills and confidence.

Summary

Chapter 4 has reviewed illustrations of facilitated self-help, selected to highlight some major features of which social workers need to be aware and to take account. From the standpoint of social workers, it has noted that facilitated self-help is most desirable in conditions where effective self-help could not survive autonomously. On the other hand, the activity can be effective without the high level of professional support and resourcing encountered in integral self-help.

5

Social Workers and Autonomous Self-Help

Although by definition autonomous self-help is located outside any social work organisation and operates independently of professionals, it is necessary for social workers to appreciate that both the range of activities and their location in relation to professional practice generates a number of opportunities for practitioners.

Nature of autonomous self-help

There is an ever-expanding number of autonomous self-help groups and organisations, ranging from the archetypal AA founded in 1935, to the most recently formed community group. The autonomy of self-help groups and organisations tends to be strongest in aspects of practice where they function as alternative to, or substitute for, professional activity. But to the extent that this statement reflects the tendency for professionals to view self-help from their own vantage point, we should avoid defining it simply as either an alternative or as a substitute for social work. Activities which are independent of social workers are no less significant, but simply are less visible to them. There is also the greater likelihood with autonomous self-help, that implicitly or explicitly it displays values and practices which do not harmonise with, or actually conflict with, social work.

So the autonomous self-help sector presents a good deal in terms of its variety with which professionals have to come to terms. The range of autonomous activity extends from settings where social workers are viewed as friendly if unrelated neighbours to those where they are seen as enemies. Whilst it may be relatively straightforward to develop ways of relating to the former, the latter represents a real challenge to the professionalism of the social worker. The very existence of autonomous self-help as external to professional practice makes it difficult to make an accurate assessment of the size of the sector and under-estimation is likely. While some autonomous groups also form a permanent feature of the network of help and support available to people, a great number are relatively short-lived. But if the field of health is representative, there has been a rapid proliferation of self-help groups in the past half century. For example, in 1940, there were fifty functioning groups of AA in the US, and by 1972 the number had grown to 18 612 (Tracy and Gussow, 1976, p. 383).

Criteria determining the relevance of autonomous self-help to social work

In the present climate of resource constraints on social workers, the most likely scenario involves autonomous self-help being seen either as a substitute for social work services or as straightforwardly complementing or supplementing them. Chapter 9 of this book tackles the risk of self-help being seen as a cheap alternative to social work. For the present, it is argued that, as a general principle, autonomous self-help should be seen as alternative to professional services only under the following conditions:

1. Where this does not imply any detrimental consequence either for the self-help activities or for the level and quality of those services
2. Where resource cutting does not accompany or follow its initiation
3. Where people's self-caring does not impair their quality of life
4. Wherever independence from professionals can be encouraged, consistent with the above
5. Where independence from, distance from and/or conflict with, the professional standpoint is intrinsic to the self-help activity.

Forms of autonomous self-help

As far as the relationship of autonomous self-help with social work
is concerned, two forms can be identified:

Self-help complementing or supplementing social work

The essential features of this form of autonomous self-help are
that it tends to form part of the continuum or network of services,
rather than primarily challenging or offering a critique of these,
although in one sense its very existence suggests a criticism of the
shortcomings of services.

A well-established example of a self-help organisation which
functions largely autonomously from social work agencies is the
Asian Resource Centre (ARC) in Birmingham, which came about
through a grassroots initiative by people involved in a multi-
cultural centre called Action Centre. Workers involved at that
time noted the need for a centre specifically designed to meet the
needs of Asians. The ARC is located in a street of shops in
Handsworth and acts as a community centre for the Asian
community, working

> in the relevant languages with a deep understanding of the religious and
> cultural aspirations of the people it serves. The services are provided
> through advice work at the Centre, running appropriate projects like
> the Asian Elders, Women's Welfare Rights, Housing Welfare, etc. and
> by providing resources and practical help in such areas as immigration,
> nationality and passport advice work, through a coherent policy of
> anti-racism and anti-sexism. The Centre produces leaflets, pamphlets in
> Asian languages and acts as a pressure group to statutory agencies. It
> provides educational and training facilities for the local community,
> voluntary and statutory agencies. The Centre is staffed by Asian
> Workers and managed by elected representatives of the Asian com-
> munity (Asian Resource Centre, 1987).

The aims of the ARC are stated as follows: first, 'to identify and
analyse the cultural and the social system placed upon particularly
disadvantaged sections of the Asian community within the neighbourhood and elsewhere, and also identify its general and specific
needs'; second, 'to initiate, participate and assist in projects
designed to protect their civil and human rights, to encourage
freedom of cultural expression and encourage all Asians to

reassert their cultural identity, self confidence and pride' (Asian Resource Centre, 1987).

The management committee of the ARC comprises eighteen people, including ten members elected by open vote at the Annual General Meeting, five who are co-opted for their particular skills and two councillors who represent the Local Authority. Its seven full-time workers are funded by the Inner City Partnership Programme, the Housing Authority, the Social Services Department, Cadbury Trust and other donations and funds. An effort is made to maintain a balanced staff team, reflecting Bengali, Pakistani and Punjabi (Indian) interests, in its broad range of community-oriented activities.

The ARC exemplifies the autonomous sector of self-help, in that it came into being as a result of the awareness of groups in the community who were aware that their needs were not being met by professionals and who were motivated to generate a self-help initiative to that end.

Self-help as an alternative to, or a substitute for, social work

Whether the group is fairly long-lived or has a limited life, the essential feature emphasised here is that it functions, implicitly or explicitly, as a critical presence in the field of helping services. That is, in relation to social work, its presence implies more or less some criticism of existing services. This critical presence may be with regard to the practice of the individual social worker, the agency, the entire service, or indeed several services.

Survivors Speak Out   One of the most apt illustrations of this form of self-help is Survivors Speak Out, an organisation which stands in the self-advocacy movement in the field of mental health.

Survivors' groups such as Survivors Speak Out include former patients such as people who have been in mental hospitals and have spread in recent years through many Western countries. Some have well-established networks of contact people, furthered in some cases by magazines or newsletters. Survivors Speak Out is a network founded in 1985 in Britain and helping individuals and groups to keep in touch with each other. Both 'system survivors' and 'allies' are working together in this organisation to develop self-advocacy. After the first national conference of users of psychiatric services in September 1987, one user said 'This weekend has been more helpful to me through mutual support than many years of medication ever were'. Another who chose to attend rather than be admitted to a psychiatric hospital said: 'My consultant wanted to admit me. I chose to come here. I can only thank everyone because coming here has done me far more good than any mental hospital ever could' (*Survivors Speak Out Newssheet*, 1988).

But such organisations expose rather than resolve contradictions embodied in the more radical practice of autonomous self-help. Chief among these contradictions is that produced between the form of self-help and the values and purposes it espouses. Thus, for instance survivors' groups such as Survivors Speak Out become affiliated to a radical agenda for change in the policy and practice of mental health, but at the same time individuals may seek basic support and help from the group itself. We can see this paradox operating more clearly in the area of women's therapy groups.

Coping with the contradictory character of radical self-help   Feminist theory has produced its own distinctive organisational forms. It is no accident that these are small groups which are not centralised or hierarchically led. Neither does the resistance to hierarchy imply a rejection of organisation itself. The stimulus has been the urge to provide structures which allow all individual women who wish to contribute their ideas to express their feelings and views, to communicate and act collectively. The political motivation for this initiative often has been self-consciously socialist (Rowbotham *et al.*, 1980, p. 40). But its development is not without dangers and dilemmas. Either the organisation could become too organised and coercive, reflecting the anxieties of group members to get something done, or it could become anarchic with members preoccupied with living a liberated life rather than concerned to develop the politics of liberation (Rowbotham *et al.*, 1980, p. 41).

Some feminists have argued that by staying in touch with their feelings women have contradicted the male view that feelings should be put down. As the founder of Women's Lib in New York City says of women's consciousness-raising groups: 'Our feelings will lead us to our theory, our theory to our action, our feelings about that action to new theory and then to action' (Sarachild, 1971, p. 159).

This does not mean that feminist therapy necessarily occupies a vacuum at the point where psychological or psychodynamic discussion might be illuminating. It is partly a question of perception and strategy in therapy: that is, how much do the problems of this or that woman reflect the social structure? How far do they illustrate her response to it and how far can she be helped to respond so as to improve her management of them? After all, feminist therapy generates a paradox since a too ready insistence that a woman's problems are brought about solely by the social structure may lead to the individual being paralysed by the belief that she can do nothing to affect her fate, determined as it is by her societal environment. So, feminist analysis may produce conditions as unencouraging to liberation as the view at the other extreme which blames the victim for her problems (Howell, 1981, p. 512).

How social workers may relate to autonomous self-help

As we saw in Chapters 1 and 2, it is not the case that all self-help groups and organisations which exist independently of social workers are necessarily critical of them. But the illustrations we have selected here demonstrate how, by its very existence, the autonomous self-help sector tends to represent a critique of social services, among many others.

Furthermore, by definition, the concept of autonomous self-help as we have defined it, implies that professionals do not intervene in what is going on. At first sight, it may seem as though there is nothing more to be said. But three main activities by social workers are appropriate, in relating to different forms of autonomous self-help.

- The *referral* to self-help activities of individuals who may benefit
- The *maintenance of constructive liaison* with activities
- The *importing to the social work setting* of learning from the self-help activities.

Referral to a group

Annie's client, Jean has a disability and has been depressed. This has seriously affected her work and her relationships. It helps Jean when Annie provides her with some information about women's groups in the area and she is then able to make a decision herself, without pressure from Annie, about whether or not she wants to try one of the groups.

The story may conclude with Annie living happily ever after. However, there may be a need for Annie to cope with the consequences which accrue for other professionals working with Jean, as a result of Jean's involvement in the group. Specifically, this arises because Annie receives some criticism from colleagues, for her support of Jean's attendance at the women's health group. Annie realises that on occasions the values of autonomous self-help activities may *conflict with* rather than *complement*, the views of professionals. They may be none the less effective for this, in providing help to people.

Maintenance of constructive liaison

After Jean has been attending the women's group for a year, she reappears in the office one day asking for help. Apparently, the group has had to close and re-open in another part of the town as a response to the loss of its premises. Annie appreciates that Jean cannot travel the extra distance to attend the group. The same colleagues who criticised the women's health group now make carping comments about its withdrawal from the locality. Annie takes this up with them strongly. The incident emphasises the importance of social workers not regarding autonomous self-help groups as a substitute for professional services for people.

Importing learning from the self-help

To the extent that a self-help group or organisation exists independently of social work, the social worker should be ready to regard it as a source of experience from which to learn. It is tempting to disregard the critique afforded by the existence of autonomous self-help and to focus even more on what is seen as one's core duties. However, the task of the sensitive and aware practitioner should be to appreciate what is being offered by autonomous self-helpers and to interpret their contribution in terms of present practice in the social work organisation.

Thus, for instance, the existence of ARC is an exhortation for social workers to examine their own practice in terms of challenging racism and developing more ethnically sensitive social work. Further, the work of Survivors Speak Out offers a critical perspective on mental health provision as it exists today.

Together, these illustrations strengthen the case for social workers not to ignore or downgrade the significance of autonomous self-help, but to take it on board as part of their ongoing critical evaluation of their own practice.

Further, perhaps the vitality and vociferousness of organisations such as Survivors Speak Out, and their critical impact even on such groups in the voluntary sector as MIND, bring home the capacity of self-help to act as a powerful agent for change. Autonomy and independence may go hand in hand with social workers feeling discomfort from the conflict between their own perspective and that of the self-helpers. Yet the very untidiness of the autonomous sector may engender creative conflict which can contribute to personal and professional growth.

Practice issues

Sustaining autonomous self-help: the awkward dilemma

Autonomous self-help needs the guarantee of reasonably long-term funding if it is to guarantee effectiveness. In effect, initiatives which for one reason or another depend on maintaining an independent, or even a critical, position in relation to surrounding agencies really should be able to receive funds without any strings attached. The reality for most groups and organisations is not as straightforward. The reality for the social worker is fraught, since by definition autonomous self-help is independent. All that we can say is that activities valued by practitioners should be nurtured by whatever means are possible, without threatening to compromise their independence. The ARC in Handsworth manages to sustain an independent ethos, despite the fact that some of its funding is contributed from agencies such as social services.

Maintaining an appreciation of the diversity of self-help

There is a need to guarantee the integrity of the autonomous sector of self-help by giving it a form of unconditional positive regard which goes beyond mere tolerance. A positive appreciation of diversity is necessary, which is the accompaniment to the self-critical relationship with it referred to above. Social workers need to encourage autonomous self-help and at the same time to learn to live with it as a continuous, critical presence.

Developing and improving social work practice

The autonomous self-help sector may have a particular contribution to make to the development of more challenging and assertive approaches by social workers to some of the injustices and aspects of oppression which are endemic, not just in society but in the profession of social work itself. Social workers thus need to look to self-help groups and organisations as additional means to promote equal opportunities policies and forms of practice which counter and challenge injustice and which are anti-discriminatory.

Summary

Chapter 5 has highlighted the conditions under which autonomous self-help is most likely to flourish, drawing attention to the circumstances likely to govern their relevance or usefulness to social workers. Particular attention has been drawn to ways in which social workers should relate to autonomous self-help, learn themselves and help their agencies learn, from such experiences.

6

Initiating and Maintaining a Self-Help Group or Organisation

Chapter 6 examines the major considerations relevant to the maintenance of self-help. We begin with some general factors which need to be born in mind by those involved either in starting an activity or in ensuring its continuance. Then we describe how a self-help group or organisation may be maintained.

How does self-help start?

Several major factors are involved in the process of getting self-help started and ensuring its effective continuance, either for a limited period or on an open-ended basis.

Finding enough self-helpers

Enough members need to be found to start an activity, yet a way may need to be found of attracting only those whose purposes are consonant with the intended activity. This begs crucial questions about mechanisms to screen potential participants in activities, whether these should exist and if so how they should be set up (Donnan and Lenton, 1985, p. 44). It also raises the issue as to whether self-help groups should have open or closed membership. Open groups generally allow new members to join at any time, while closed groups allow no more members to join after they have reached an agreed size.

The screening process may be either formal or informal. Formal procedures may involve discussions or meetings between founding or existing participants. Intending participants may be given information about the activities as a whole or about other participants and in return may be expected to provide some information. The choice as to whether to attend may be left with the new participant or be made in a meeting by all the existing participants. The existing participants may accept new participants once and for all, or in the case of some therapeutically-oriented groups may require each to go through a number of probationary or trial meetings.

In general, the more restrictions the existing participants impose on potential participants, the more limited is the pool of potential participants. However, the very need for participants to retain a sharp focus on a narrowly defined task may necessitate the insistence on an entry requirement, as in the case of an autonomous women's group dealing with sexual abuse or rape, which excludes professionals and men.

Finding a place to meet

Ideally, activities should take place in a setting which unites participants by virtue of their common experience. In the medical group studied by Bond *et al.* (1976), the fact that meetings occurred in the hospital clearly fulfilled this requirement. In many facilitated and autonomous activities, though, it will be neither feasible nor desirable for participants to share an experience which relates in some way to the purpose of their meeting, in this fashion.

Ensuring adequate publicity

Undoubtedly, the participation of people in self-help activities depends initially on adequate publicity being given to planned events and subsequently on the establishment of effective means of communication. In some instances, groups rely on word of mouth communication once meetings have become routinised. Others produce newsletters where membership of an organisation or group is more scattered and activities do not necessarily take the form of face to face group meetings. The use of a variety of media may improve the image of an activity and enable potential participants, the general public and professionals such as social workers to receive information about it. Robinson and Henry's study of self-help groups in the health field, based on members' own accounts, identifies three factors as important in their origins: the failure of existing services, the recognition of the value of mutual help, and the role of the media (Robinson and Henry, 1977, p. 12).

The issue of successful publicity is inseparable from that of resources. It may be necessary to produce posters, advertisements, leaflets or a newspaper article before a core of active participants has been generated, who would be able to help to resource them. We have seen in Chapter 4 how the social worker may use the publicity arising from the typical experience of an individual, either in a newspaper article or a leaflet, to raise public concern when a local group is being founded.

Guaranteeing adequate support

Bond notes the usefulness of a notice board which helps to support local groups as well as promoting the entire organisation. But the group he is studying may be unusually structured, for he describes the notice board as displaying guidelines, training and opportunities for contacts with more established chapters, by which he means other local groups. His example of self-help is a federated structure of local groups within an established framework. As he says,

> The corporate structure also provides public relations information, organises workshops and conducts the national convention, providing broader opportunities for all members to become involved in the large-scale development of the organisation (Bond *et al.*, 1979, p. 60).

But while a corporate structure may be a bonus for some groups, many flourish without it. Indeed there is something to be said for an organisation which is loose enough for each local group to develop an autonomous local identity, purely as a reflection of its members' interests, preferences and needs.

Achieving legitimacy

'Legitimacy' concerns the credibility or acceptability of an activity in the eyes of relevant people, including participants and professionals, where appropriate. The group Bond studied gained legitimacy through the active support of professionals such as doctors. However, in the range of self-help considered in Chapters 3–5, the issue of legitimacy is much broader.

The way a self-help activity is run is crucial to its maintenance. Knight and Hayes (1981, pp. 83–4) suggest that social and recreational activities may help to improve the credibility of a self-help group with potential members. Local people should also be involved in management, to the extent of employing them alongside other professionals wherever possible.

All self-help activities need to maintain a degree of credibility both with existing and potential participants, as well as with relevant professionals where this is important to the participants. Clearly, acceptability to professionals is not a requirement for every group's survival. In instances of self-help functioning as complementary with professional services, the sympathy or support of professionals may be valuable. Where self-help operates as an alternative to, or as competitor with, existing services, of necessity distance from professionals will be maintained.

Support from professionals makes a positive difference. Unell observes that 100 per cent of new initiatives given professional support in the Nottingham Self-Help Project led to groups being established, in contrast with about 40 per cent of those given limited or no support (Unell, 1987, p. 37). However, in the light of our consideration of autonomous activity in Chapter 5, we can speculate that these may have been a self-defining sample of groups needing some facilitation. On the whole, autonomous self-help gains its legitimacy either independently of professionals, or by contrasting itself with them. It is important for social workers not to deny to self-helpers this right to distinguish themselves clearly from the aura of professional practice.

Recruiting helpers

In the group Bond studied, the recruitment process was helped particularly by existing members visiting potential new members in connection with the serious surgical operations that were being carried out on them.

The success of initiatives often depends largely on the ability of participants to make connections at the right pace and at the appropriate time between people who would form supportive chains in aspects crucial to the survival of these projects.

Potential members of self-help groups and organisations may be thought to be mainly articulate and middle-class. But this varies very much from setting to setting. Some organisations, like the Humberside Project (Chapter 3) recruit predominantly working-class participants by virtue of their location. Others find that their membership covers a wide social class spectrum. In an admittedly small-scale survey of mental health self-help groups associated with the Mind Your Self project in 1984, in one group a university researcher, semi-skilled and unskilled unemployed members were found (Lindenfield and Adams, 1984, pp. 24–5).

Nevertheless, somehow at the start, self-help activities need a push. As Knight and Hayes (1981, p. 88) put it: 'To get started groups need highly motivated, articulate and numerate individuals to hold frequent meetings to mount campaigns of action'.

Maintaining involvement

A self-help activity needs to involve sufficient participants to enable the programme to proceed. The impetus of each activity will be improved to the extent that participants have a personal stake in it. Whilst the success of a programme as a whole may be problematic in the sense that it remains a matter of opinion and experience, the maintenance of each activity depends on more objective criteria such as a certain minimum level of attendance and participation by members.

The circumstances of newcomers to self-help groups are similar in some ways to those of new volunteers in social welfare organisations, who originally seek personal help, but more often than not shift to getting satisfaction from helping others (Katz, 1970, p. 60). In other words, people participate in self-help because they are getting something out of it. In the early stages, recruits may receive more than they contribute and later on the balance between help received and help given may be rather different.

The effectiveness of involvement of participants depends on how well activities are managed. Group meetings in particular need effective leaders (Lindenfield and Adams, 1984, p. 33). On the whole, a democratic style of leadership is preferred to authoritarian or laissez faire approaches (Lindenfield and Adams, 1984, pp. 34–5). Some people argue that larger groups benefit from having two or more leaders working together, but Preston-Shoot considers this too simplistic and examines the conditions under which it would be appropriate (Preston-Shoot, 1987, Chapter 4).

More substantial advice on running meetings can be found in handbooks such as that by Holloway and Otto (1986). Integrity Groups have also produced guidelines for the conduct of effective group meetings (Mowrer, 1972, p. 27).

It is tidy, but misleading, to assume that self-help activities are coterminus with the sum total of members' self-help and self-care. It is quite common to find members developing relationships within their group which generate a variety of extra-group activities. In informal, social, leisure and other areas, relationships, projects and friendships develop out of meetings, sustain them and are sustained by them.

It is a short step from this process to consider the notion that groups may be open-ended rather than time limited. In contrast with many contract-linked therapeutic areas of a more formal or traditional nature, self-help activities generally do not have the same concern with limited involvement in the helping process. By the same token, members of groups may not set their sights so much on total cure or release from problems as the outcome of activities, as upon the week by week management of those problems as the group proceeds. In other words, membership of a particular group may become a way of life.

Associated with this broadening of relationships between self-helpers is the issue of confidentiality. Some self-help groups actually have rules forbidding members to discuss business relating to the group outside meetings. This underlines the need for participants to clarify the boundaries of their relationships with, and responsibilities to, each other. In this regard, the illustration of the work of the RSSPCC in Chapter 3 is instructive.

Securing sufficient resources

Self-help activities, groups, programmes and organisations draw their resources from a wide variety of sources. Some larger organisations seek and obtain large grants from statutory bodies, nationally or locally. In the US, Parents Anonymous has received over one million dollars, the bulk of its donations, in Federal grants (Borman, 1979, p. 40).

Advice on getting grants is succinctly expressed by a joint working party of the Association of Metropolitan Authorities (AMA), the National Council for Voluntary Organisations (NCVO) and the Association of County Councils (ACC) (Jones, 1981, Chapters 2–4). Advice on employing people is in the publication by Sheila Kurowska (1984). Effective integral and facilitated self-help activity may benefit from a written agreement, defining the essential elements of the relationship between professionals and self-helpers. Recent advice on such contracts contains sufficient arguments in favour of them to overcome most of the doubts of the faint-hearted (Jones, 1981, pp. 9–11 and there is a model contract in Appendix 5 of that volume). One particularly useful tip from the working party concerns the advantages of leaving the detailed scheduling of activities out of the document, so that these can be modified separately without affecting the overall agreement, in subsequent reviews (Jones, 1981, p. 10). Obviously, such written agreements do not in themselves resolve issues which have not been sorted out elsewhere. As the working party conclude: 'Contracts themselves do not create mutual trust. Rather they are the products of such trust' (Jones, 1981, p. 11).

The relevance of agreements is in their public relations value to self-helpers who need to establish credibility with potential sources of resources, of whatever kind. They demonstrate to others the capacity to relate positively and easily, the capacity to work effectively with professionals and subsequently they may even be used to show that the resources and effort have been used in a worthwhile way. The features of successful consultation arrangements between statutory and voluntary bodies have been noted by the working party referred to above (Jones, 1981, pp. 28–9).

Money is not the sole, or even the main, resource for the small, local self-help group, which may depend on having somewhere to meet and the facilities to make tea or coffee during meetings. A minimum of administrative support, such as the means of making posters or leaflets, may be vital also to enable the group to get started. The location of meetings may be crucial, for the setting influences largely the tone of meetings. Some self-help groups will have the offer of subsidised or free accommodation; some will meet in members' homes to avoid any contact with professional premises; others will hire a room to ensure meetings take place as far as possible on neutral territory.

Caution should be exercised wherever possible to ensure safeguards against loss of resourcing. For instance, self-help groups or organisations may grow to the point where they look self-supporting. In other words, self-helpers and professionals involved with them need to appreciate the risks of becoming too successful in other people's eyes.

Dealing with difficult situations

Conceptualisations of group processes may underplay references to problems and crises which can be so major as to lead to the premature demise of an activity. It is worth noting that participants in activities need the necessary knowledge and skills to enable them to deal with such areas as people whose problems tend to dominate and exclude consideration of other essential matters. Additionally, participants in activities may need to be able to cope with each other's sadness as well as anger and, in extreme circumstances, even violence (Lindenfield and Adams, 1984, Chapter 5, Preston-Shoot, 1987, pp. 105–10). Furthermore, some self-help initiatives can be put at risk by the tendency for an individual or small clique to dominate a group or organisation. Other participants need to possess the necessary skills to assert control in such circumstances and maintain the purpose of the activity. The handling of conflict in groups is dealt with in Lindenfield and Adams (1984, Chapter 5) and that between organisations in Jones (1981, pp. 35–6).

Participants need their quota of resilience to deal with difficulties like these, as well as with the ultimate problem of the failure of an activity, not losing hope but restarting and continuing.

How are self-help activities maintained?

Sourcebooks for practice

There are many handbooks which offer step by step advice to initiators of self-help groups. For instance, in the US. Donnan and Lenton (1985) have written for individual women as well as for groups facilitators, Phyllis Silverman (1980) has rooted her advice in research as well as personal experience and Judy Wilson has discussed the practicalities for self-help (1986) and carers' (1988) groups in Britain. In fifteen perceptive pages, Liz Evans *et al.* (1986, Chapters 6 and 7) gives advice to carers such as parents of handicapped children on setting up and running self-help groups.

Knight and Hayes observe, in the light of studying thirty community self-help groups, that the very characteristics of strong leadership by articulate individuals which help to establish them are likely to inhibit their subsequent development (Knight and Hayes 1981, p. 88). The maintenance of activities which involve local people depends subsequently on reducing the emphasis on bureaucratic activity, formal meetings, reducing dependence on middle class and/or professional leadership and developing social events alongside the other purposes of the group or activities.

Key questions

While it may be useful to draw on such handbooks for particular initiatives, for our purposes it is helpful to stand back behind the technicalities of running a group and develop a framework which encompasses different approaches to the processes of self-help. Although the stages of group life may be conceptualised (Preston-Shoot, 1987, pp. 111–19), there is no guarantee that all groups will necessarily pass through these, or in any case experience them in a common sequence.

Katz (1970) suggests that self-help organisations move through five stages in their life-histories: origins, informal organisation, the emergence of leadership, beginning of formal organisation, and the appointment of paid staff and professional workers. We have dealt with the factors involved in the early stages of self-help in the previous section, so for the purposes of brevity we can coalesce the first two stages indicated by Katz under the heading of 'founding'.

How is the group or organisation founded? It is paradoxical that founders of self-help groups and organisations so often have been professionals. In six out of ten organisations studied, Borman found that professionals played a key part in founding and early development (Borman, 1979, p. 21). Some self-help groups and organisations have been started by former members of other organisations. Thus, Synanon was founded by a former member of AA and this helps to explain the similarities in the purposes and operating principles of those two organisations. Often, those founding self-help organisations seek advice, either from someone involved in an existing activity or from sympathetic professionals, such as social workers, doctors, clergy, educationalists, workers in voluntary agencies and others.

It is common for participants in self-help activities at the birth of the group or organisation to experience anxiety or panic about the future of the self-help initiative itself (Lindenfield and Adams, 1984, p. 20). This is in addition to any anxieties experienced in connection with the problem or issue for which self-help is sought. In part, this is the reason why in the very early stages many people give up and many young self-help initiatives perish.

At the community level, organisational factors may weigh heavily in the founding days of a self-help initiative. The examples quoted in Chapter 3 involve partnerships between self-helpers and professionals. In the cases of integral and facilitated self-help, three factors identified in respect of effective partnership in social service can be applied here. First, there are questions of ideology reflected in the attitude of the local authority agencies towards involvement with the voluntary sector; second, there is the availability of resources from sources such as local authority departments and central government; thirdly, there is the degree of priority given by the local authority to the area or client group served by the voluntary body (Jones, 1981, pp. 6–7).

What sort of leadership emerges? In the early days, it is not only the new member but also the group itself which is vulnerable. Despite the fact that in the early stages members may be very enthusiastic, this enthusiasm can evaporate very quickly if certain basic requirements are not met. The bread-and-butter of organising and leading meetings, for instance, is no less crucial because its importance is obvious. What distinguishes many self-help initiatives from professional ones often is the way in self-help the task of leadership is shared by several people. It is commonly said that effective groups are democratically led. But in self-help the knowledge and skills which underpin this leadership need to be demonstrated by a sufficient number of participants in order to sustain a broad consensus about group goals, a good level of communication and a degree of participation which gives all those involved an appropriate stake in what is going on (Lindenfield and Adams, 1984, p. 22).

Knight and Hayes give advice on the emergence and growth of self-help community groups (1981, Chapter 6). New projects, they suggest, often need external help since community groups are in competition with other aspects of people's lives, people tend to adjust on an individualistic basis to problems and without a common objective and deprivation itself may have an inhibiting effect on collective action. Additionally, political experience, knowledge and skill in running organisations and negotiating for resources are required (Knight and Hayes, 1981, p. 77). The argument that increasing state provision of services induces dependence, passivity and a decline in self-help and mutual aid, is well-discussed and presents the potentially disastrous temptation to cut social provision in order to increase voluntary participation (Knight and Hayes, 1981, p. 78).

On the contrary, the key to the problem may be seen as to increase the effectiveness of reticulists. Knight and Hayes define 'reticulists' (1981, p. 50) as young, middle-class, articulate and socially and politically committed. Whilst they may succeed in initiating groups, this may perpetuate the elitist tendency for such people to retain leadership of activities which ideally might have been owned and run by poor and deprived people (Knight and Hayes, 1981, p. 79).

Will a formal self-help organisation emerge?   Unlike many organisations, self-help initiatives do not invariably pass beyond the first stage of their founding to a more formal organisational stage. The initial founders do not automatically hand over to professional administrators. In this respect, Borman's study (1979) stands in sharp contrast with the earlier work of Katz. None of the ten groups Borman studied developed comparably with Katz's groups. Nevertheless, Borman reports (Borman, 1979, p. 41) that Katz later found (Katz and Bender, 1976, p. 122) that the growth of formal organisation and professionalism were not universal features of self-help groups.

Perhaps the reason for this seemingly obstinate refusal of self-help groups to behave like emergent formal organisations is the simple fact that they differ from them in major ways. Not least, autonomous self-help initiatives in particular differ in that they are founded by lay members and many later retain their local, small-scale character. Obviously, exceptions such as AA are significant, if only because they stand out as exceptions to the great mass of small initiatives which live and die at a very local level. At a bureaucratic extreme perhaps, Mended Hearts, a medical self-help organisation, has grown to mimic the kind of organisation self-help often sets out to shun. Bond comments that

> as self-help groups become large organisations, it is more difficult for new individuals to become personally involved in the group's core activities. The large formal meetings lead most participants to view themselves as an audience. For members who are not involved in a help-giving capacity (that is, non-visitors), perceived benefits of group membership are minimal, and their peripheral involvement in the organisation is underscored (Bond *et al.*, 1979, p. 59).

At a more modest level, it is easy to see how groups planning more than one meeting at a time move towards a division of the labour which this involves, from chairing and administering, to taking notes of decisions, writing letters and acting as treasurer or caterer. Not many groups survive without at least finding reliable ways of distributing these tasks and ensuring they are carried out responsibly.

How will self-help develop into helping others?   Another way in which a self-help group may develop is through the original group changing its focus from an inward-directed orientation towards issues directly affecting participants, to a more outward-directed view. This may be achieved by inviting outsiders, such as speakers or students, to contribute to meetings (Lindenfield and Adams, 1984, p. 95). Clearly the presence of an outsider changes the character of a group and may have a dramatic impact, turning the participants towards some new activity or in an unexpected direction.

A group or organisation may reach the stage where members become involved in educational events as part of their role in the group, although members of less well-established groups may be less likely to do this. They may need encouragement from others. Courses and conferences may happen, to which a group can send representatives. Such events often will welcome non-professionals and some will reduce fees for members of self-help groups. A grant may be obtained for attendance at a training course. The local Council for Voluntary Service (CVS) or Adult Education Centre may make provision for people to be sponsored on such a course. Topics on such courses may include coping with depression, issues of race and gender, raising children alone, unemployment and finding work, looking after elderly people, voluntary action and, last but not least, running self-help activities.

Involvement in local community or wider issues comes more easily to some groups than to others. Some groups may be more used to taking up issues than others, for instance by becoming involved in activities which raise community awareness, through some form of information gathering locally or an educational campaign concerning a health issue. As time passes, some groups or organisations develop outside activities to the point where their resources begin to stimulate the growth of other helping activities in the community. While some groups, notably consciousness-raising groups, have this more or less built into their aims, others may move towards it slowly and with difficulty. Those involved may need the encouragement of a ready-provided rationale.

Three justifications can be given. First, those who have met to help themselves and each other have demonstrated already their commitment and motivation and may have reached the point where they would be stimulated by, and help others through, a wider focus for their efforts. Second, self-help groups need to avoid becoming insular and should benefit from keeping in touch with local developments. Third, groups may find it fruitful to encourage and support other people who are interested in self-help but have not yet taken the plunge (Lindenfield and Adams, 1984, p. 94). But the growth of formal organisation is not predicated upon outside activities. They are used here as an example of typical developments which would produce pressure towards it.

Clearly, another positive direction in which self-helpers may move is towards more overt community work. Alan Twelvetrees (1982) and Paul Henderson (Henderson and Thomas, 1980, pp. 148–86) have commented on the stages involved in the process of community work. Twelvetrees identifies eight stages in work with community groups:

1. Contacting people and analysing needs
2. Bringing people together, helping them to identify needs and developing the will to meet those needs
3. Adopting objectives
4. Creating a suitable organisation to this end
5. Helping them to form a plan of action
6. Helping them divide and carry out the consequent tasks
7. Helping them to feed results of the action, evaluate and adopt fresh objectives in the light of this.
8. The final stage comes at the point where the participants themselves take on the repetition of these last two stages and the facilitator withdraws (Twelvetrees, 1982, p. 39).

Can paid or professional staff be employed by self-helpers? Although it is difficult to generalise about its nature and timing, there does seem to be a point where the increasing outward-directedness of some self-help groups and organisations pushes participants towards establishing a formal organisation, with all that implies. This may sound as though it contradicts the principles of self-help, but it is easy to see how self-helpers move towards it.

How should self-helpers handle difficulties A number of difficulties may arise in the running of self-help groups and organisations. These are evident in the form of leadership problems, personality clashes and all the multitude of niggling hiccups which seem to beset meetings and activities in any group from time to time. We can see these generally in terms of the power struggles which go on in such circumstances: people vying for attention and for control, within themselves and between one another.

An issue of power? Thus, we emphasise the need for all to take responsibility for the social health of the group or organisation. As far as possible, members should strive to maintain a healthy balance between tolerating creative imbalances of power, conflicts and clashes and keeping them within reasonable limits. It is important not to see conflict necessarily as a sign that all is not well in the group. Many groups thrive on conflict. The important thing is that members feel they are gaining something from the meetings and other activities.

But however creative conflict is, it can be very harmful if it is not dealt with effectively when it arises. On the whole, it is usually more helpful than not for conflicts to be brought out into the open by means of members sharing their different feelings and views, in much the way that we suggest they *review the activity* (see below).

The response to disruptive individuals should also be neither to ignore them nor to panic! Usually, the reason for the behaviour of the person who disrupts by talking too much, interrupting or shouting, becoming aggressive or violent, can be seen quite quickly, if we ask ourselves the question 'why are they seeking attention/exercising power in this way?'

Sometimes it is sufficient for the meeting to be suspended while time is given to this person. The time spent can be rewarded by them settling down quickly. Others may need to talk about their feelings outside the meeting. Some may decide that these self-help meetings are not for them. It is important for the social worker, as it is for other self-helpers, to accept that the self-help activity is not beneficial to everybody. Some people may need counselling out of it.

It is important also to recognise that disruption to the activity should not necessarily be seen as though it is the responsibility of one person. There is a danger in self-help groups, as in all groups, of one person becoming the butt of the bad feelings of others. This scapegoated person may be perceived as disruptive when in fact there are imbalances in the way other people are relating to each other, which may need serious and careful examination before proceeding further.

The reciprocal of the symptomatic disruptiveness referred to above is apathetic behaviour by one or more members. This may take the form of silence, non-participation or simply staying away from meetings. In many ways, everything we have said about handling aggressive behaviour or conflict situations applies here. However, it is always worth bearing in mind that the situation can be improved dramatically, simply by introducing some new stimulation into the meeting, such as an exercise involving physical movement, or a social break for people to make hot drinks and chat for a while.

How should self-helpers handle endings? We should not assume that the self-help process is open-ended for everybody. Many people gain a good deal from their experience and finish their contact with an agency, group or organisation there and then. Both for individuals and groups, there is a need to consider endings as a common and natural stage in the process of self-help. This needs stating more strongly in the face of the tendency for self-help groups to be more often open-ended and ongoing than some other forms of helping based upon professional resources. But, ironically, it also needs emphasising for the opposite reason that many self-help initiatives are short-lived, for all kinds of reasons (Lindenfield and Adams, 1984, pp. 53–5). Finally, we should avoid assuming that there is some inbuilt normative rationality about such endings, which makes everything always turn out for the best. The reasons for the closure of a self-help group are various and complex:

> It may have achieved what its members set out for it to achieve, it may want to amalgamate with another group, it may be prevented from further meetings, or the interaction between members may lead to its prompt, even sudden, closure (Lindenfield and Adams, 1984, p. 55).

Three types of ending are mentioned here, from which different permutations of individual and collective ending can be extended:

(a) **The end of the activity or meeting** Essentially, this ending should not come as a surprise to any of its participants and all should have the chance to prepare for it in advance. The more some sort of structure is adhered to, with pre-set starting and finishing times for meetings, the more likely it is that members will be able to anticipate the ending and retain control of their situation in the process. It helps if one or more members who are sharing leadership roles in the activity can take on the task of bringing explicitly to people's attention the fact that the meeting will be finishing in, say, ten minutes' time.

The actual closing of the meeting can be preceded with some form of stocktaking activity. It may be sufficient to go round the entire group asking for comments. Or a more structured exercise may be preferred, with members writing one good and one bad feeling about what has happened on pieces of paper, which are folded and put into a box, then taken out, read and discussed without identifying the author of each. The latter course can be frustrating if sufficient time is not allowed to read out and talk about all the slips of paper.

(b) Where the individual wishes to end her or his contact with the self-help group or organisation   The conditions in which people stop taking part vary tremendously. Some attend but overtly do not seem to participate, then stop attending with no warning or explanation. Others announce their intention in advance. All that can be done here is to note that if members announce their intention in advance, then clearly this signals the appropriateness of a response from other members.

First, it may be productive to check out with the individual whether she or he wants to talk about the reasons for leaving. The motive for saying 'I am leaving' may have to do with drawing the attention of other people. There may be some personal reason, such as an emergency or trauma, illness or accident. There may be a conflict with another group member. Sadness or unhappiness may contribute to the wish to withdraw. Each of these needs dealing with by other members of the group. The effectiveness of the self-help activity at such times depends on those participating maintaining a sufficiently secure and supportive atmosphere to enable the issues to be explored and worked through.

(c) Where the group or organisation is closing   A surprisingly high proportion of self-help groups and organisations cease after a few meetings. It is important for the social worker to reassure people that this is normal and desirable, as long as members themselves desire it!

Self-help groups can come to an end because they have run their course, members have dropped away, most members feel the activities have achieved their objectives or people are joining other groups and organisations.

In all such circumstances, it may make sense to try to mark the occasion in some positive way. An extra lift can be given to the last meeting, by members discussing at the previous meeting how they can bring along refreshments to turn the event into a party. Or, alternatively, the party can be separated from the regular series of meetings and held on a different occasion, leaving the last meeting for more 'serious' business to do with the purpose of the self-help activity. There will usually be a good deal to review and there may be benefit in people sharing plans, in the light of their experiences together.

The activity of reviewing can be carried out systematically, along the lines of the closure of the meeting described above. It may make sense to expand this activity, depending on the length of time the activity has been running, the intensity of the experience and so on. Sometimes group members get together to write newsletters, articles, take photographs of such activities. It all depends on the degree of confidentiality and the extent of warm memories engendered by the experience. Some groups end rather suddenly, in the wake of unforeseeable difficulties. Others end on a high note with hugs and mutual thanks all round.

Summary

In Chapter 6, we have provided a checklist of essential considerations for those wanting to get involved in initiating and/or maintaining self-help. At the same time, we have drawn attention to relevant issues which arise in the actual process of running self-help activities.

7

How to Appraise Self-Help

In Chapter 7, we consider the sequence that the appraisal of self-help activities will invariably move through and the kinds of issues and questions which normally will need to be addressed in the process. The major stages are as follows: clarifying the task, preparing for the appraisal, carrying it out and producing and using its products. It should be remembered that far from each stage being completed before the next is begun, in practice constant 'looping back' will normally be necessary, to revise the task of appraisal and its implementation.

Clarifying the task

'Appraisal' describes the attempt to feed back to people answers to questions they pose about what they are doing, how they are doing it and how 'well' they are doing it. On the whole, the sort of appraisal which those involved in self-help will encounter is concerned with the present or the immediate past rather than with the future. That is, the most common question to which an answer will be sought by means of appraisal is: 'how have we been doing in this activity?' But the equally important sequel should be 'what does this mean?' and then 'so what!' or 'what do we do now?'

We have to start by asking what the rationale is for appraising a particular self-help activity. Is it absolutely essential for some purpose, desirable, or merely contemplated out of interest?

Appraisal is not simply a major means of ensuring a rational process of decision-making concerning the future of a project or activity. Very rarely, as Key *et al.* (1976, p. 31) notes, is appraisal actually given this degree of prominence by policy-makers or managers. More realistically, the results of appraisal can be presented as one among many sources of information which all of us – private individuals, self-helpers, professionals and agency managers – may draw on when we make our decisions. The actual and honest rationale for evaluating a self-help activity may be different from the justification presented in public. But for all that, it is still crucial for the appraisal to be carried out as well as possible.

Appraisal as an empowering tool

A more positive way to view the process and the outcome of appraisal of a self-help activity is that, used sensitively and constructively, it can be a means of empowering both self-helpers and social workers. It should not be used so as to perpetuate the oppression of those in whose interests it is allegedly carried out!

For whom are we doing it? All sorts of people may be receivers of the appraisal. It may be carried out for professionals, for self-helpers, for agency funders or managers, for a mixture of these or for other people altogether such as journalists, students or academics doing independent research.

Source of sponsorship The source of sponsorship or commissioning will affect the nature of the audience for which any report is eventually written (see the section on 'producing and using the appraisal' below). It also affects how quickly they expect results. Generally speaking, academics expect results far less quickly than practitioners, so it is as well for the accountability of the evaluator as evaluator to be specified clearly at the outset, with the agreement of all stakeholders in the appraisal.

Who controls the appraisal?

We can simplify the question of control by contrasting the traditional situation, where the researcher has total control and no-one else affects the appraisal, with the consultative situation, where the researcher and the self-helpers collaborate at every stage in the process of answering all of the questions laid out in this chapter. On the whole, the more consultative the appraisal, the more time-consuming the process of continually meeting to carry it out collaboratively, but the more rewarding for all parties the sense of joint ownership of the eventual results (Patton, 1982, pp. 55–98).

Unfortunately, there is a noticeable lack of evaluative studies of self-help groups. Within the last fifteen years it has been noted that 'to date, not a single adequate study of the effectiveness of self-help groups exists' (Lieberman and Borman, 1976, p. 459). The fact that in Britain this is still largely true should not deter the practitioner at this stage.

What sort of appraisal is sought?

As we saw above, clarifying who are the sponsors and the audience helps to clarify the kind of research envisaged. Between them, they are likely to be interested in questions generated here for the sake of illustration, from within one or more of the following categories selected from those listed by Patton (1982, p. 44):

Front-end analysis

- Is there evidence in advance to justify starting a self-help activity?
- Are local conditions such that self-help activity is feasible?
- Are there enough potential self-helpers in this field in this locality?

Formative appraisal

- What activities are going on?
- What is the story of self-help in action, in this particular setting?
- What needs to be done in order to improve this programme of self-help?

Impact or summative evaluation

- What effects and outcomes has this self-help activity had?
- What is its basic worth?

The distinction between hard-line and soft-line approaches (Key *et al.*, 1976, pp. 10–11) is useful. The former rely more on the notions of scientific evaluation we might encounter in the world of business while the latter are more concerned with impressionistic, subjective or experience-based.

The preferred approach: critical appraisal

This is the term we used to cover both formative and summative studies of self-help activities in the list above. It may also be called a *case study* approach. The preference for it is based partly on grounds of the time and other resource constraints which are likely to rule out more full-blooded approaches to evaluation. But in addition, there is a real danger that evaluations of this kind could intimidate self-helpers and put them into a relatively passive and powerless situation.

A case study involves the following:

1. It is flexible, in that research questions, goals, hypotheses can be altered as the study proceeds
2. It generally involves the researcher in some kind of relatively unstructured observation
3. It invariably necessitates the researcher using her or his own reactions to a situation as a source of data, further reflection and evaluative activity
4. It is geared to understanding the process of the activity rather than pronouncing after it has finished, on the outcomes.

The process of carrying out a case study necessitates:

1. Getting access to the evidence – i.e., being patient while people get familiar enough to begin to share confidences; being around often enough and/or long enough to get a feel of what is going on
2. Looking for typical, as well as rare or unusual cases, situations, incidents, processes; trying to compare, contrast and understand these
3. Maintaining a sense of theoretical issues raised by the research
4. Keeping in touch with the sources of evidence throughout
5. Remaining open to fresh ideas and interpretations.

What is being appraised?

Is the subject of appraisal a short-lived activity which took place some weeks or months ago, on which retrospective information is sought? Is it current or planned at some time in the near future? Is the target of appraisal a single or several settings? Is it a newly established or a well-established setting, with a single, local, intermittent base or a national network of federated groups?

These questions about the character, scope and scale of the appraisal greatly affect the nature of the research devised.

Preparing for the appraisal

In general, the approach to appraisal should be sufficiently flexible to capture the unexpected and yet be sufficiently specific to enable reasonably precise, objective and valid assessments to be made.

Sources of information

Will a single individual or group be used as source, or a sample of groups? Will one kind of source be sought, or a variety of sources? The choice here is between aiming at depth of cover from one kind of source, or trying to achieve corroboration of the evidence from more than one direction, by using different sources.

Appraisal may also be considered from a vantage point *outside the activity*. For instance, the extinction of the original problem may in theory be marked by the group itself coming to an end. So, far from determining the effectiveness of self-help in terms of the number of new activities or groups which come into existence, or the length of time they have been in existence, it may be more relevant to monitor the number of groups which expire. But this itself is problematic, since activities may finish because participants become frustrated or bored, or through ineffective leadership or the intransigence of problems of one or more participants.

How much information to collect?

Clearly, the argument about whether collecting data from surveys of larger numbers of people is preferable to small-scale work can be settled in practical terms by the constraints on time which prevent many appraisals becoming large-scale. But there is a positive argument also for small numbers or even single case studies. Patton puts the point forcibly:

> It is worth remembering that some of the major breakthroughs in knowledge have come from studies with small sample sizes. Freud's work was based on a few clinical cases. Piaget significantly changed educational thinking about how children learn with an in-depth study of two children – his own (Patton, 1982, p. 219).

We may criticise Patton's choice of illustrations, but the case for very small-scale case studies is still valid, based on the high pay-off which can be achieved in terms of scope of information and qualitative depth.

Two pieces of advice need to be borne in mind:

- Don't collect too much data. It will only clutter up your filing cabinet and eventually, long after you have failed to use it, find its way into the rubbish basket
- Keep in mind the need to write a short, concise report and collect evidence to this end, and not for the sake of collecting it.

What evidence will be collected?

The great validity of ways of gathering evidence – from surveys, questionnaires and interviews of a more or less structured kind, to direct observation of activities – affects the kinds of evidence collected. Johnston Birchall convincingly argues that case histories of co-operative practice, which – although he studies housing – is very similar in character to many self-help initiatives, may be evaluated in terms of six key variables (Birchall, 1988, pp. 162–88). Adapting these to the self-help field produces the following useful list:

1. *Participation*: including 'true believers' who willingly participate, 'freeloaders' who like to benefit without sharing the costs of participating 'sceptical conformers' who conform without participating actively, 'holdouts' who refuse to con-

form but remain in the activity and 'escapees' who would leave
if given half a chance
2. *Extensity*: the size of the group and its geographical concentra-
tion
3. *Duration*: the time the group has existed
4. *Adequacy*: the ability of participants to reach the common
goals
5. *Intensity*: the depth of commitment participants have to each
other
6. *Purity*: the commitment of participants to the principles of the
activity.

A direct indication of the value of activities to people can be
obtained simply by asking them about the experience. From the
participant's point of view, the success of self-help may be seen in
terms of whether she or he feels better or happier, or more in
control of everyday life, whether esteem has increased, whether
personal relationships have improved and whether the activity has
been enjoyable. Undoubtedly, such information is hard to validate
on an objective basis, independently of the judgements of participants themselves. But it remains part of a widespread movement
which treats the way participants define their situation as the
paramount source of data on group effectiveness.

Another approach is to examine the quality of life of participants, in such major areas as work, leisure and unemployment,
relationships and family experiences. A further aspect of the focus
on the experience of participants is to compare people who seek
self-help and those who don't.

In these circumstances, the key question is what motivates some
people to take part, whether the factors concerned reflect differ-
ences in the circumstances of individuals in social or in psychological terms.

Problems of information gathering

There may be a conflict at the outset between the values of the
researcher and those of people involved in self-help. At the very
least this may lead to members of self-help activities being
unwilling to co-operate in research. They may refuse to talk about
themselves or to provide written information. They may refuse to

allow the researcher access to their activities, to gather any kind of direct evidence to enable corroboration with documentary data. This is particularly likely in the case of autonomous activities. Penny Webb's attempt to monitor a scheme designed to stimulate the setting up of self-help groups encountered problems of this kind, some people being unwilling to fill in questionnaires and others were unable to cope with them (Webb, 1982, p. 125). Lieberman and Borman (1976, p. 461) found that groups were resistant to outsiders intruding on their activities.

The values of the self-help activities may conflict with the more traditional helping activities with which researchers may wish to compare them. Thus, what many other professionals may see as the very idiosyncratic values of some self-help activities may further inhibit the straightforward appraisal of their effectiveness. It has been said that unlike psychotherapy, which emphasises honesty and self-understanding, self-help groups may encourage denial and the construction of mythologies (Lieberman and Bond, 1978, p. 229). In other words, just as some would argue that the doctor has an interest in writing a prescription in a form which mystifies the lay person and preserves professional power and mystique, so it may be argued that the alternative practitioner of self-help may develop a similar defence, albeit from a very different perspective.

Is the evaluator more interested in the *process* or in the *outcome* of the self-help activity? Who else has questions to ask? What other stakeholders have an interest, actually or potentially, in the appraisal of the activity? Whose questions have the prior claim? These are questions which concern the political and ethical dimensions of the activity. Generally speaking, there are no clear, easy or unchanging answers to them.

There are also questions of focus, which bear on the evaluative approach adopted. For instance, whereas approaches which emphasise the process bring out aspects such as the quality of the experience, those which focus on outcomes of self-help tend to highlight its impact on participants and comparisons with the impact of other kinds of activity. These issues are affected by the vantage point from which the appraisal is carried out, whether inside the activity, outside it, or a mixture of both.

Is the person doing the appraisal a part of the action, or a total outsider? Is she or he an experienced researcher, or a novice? Is she or he a professional, or a lay person going it alone, or a worker, or a student receiving a regular relevant supervision and support? Has this person an interest to declare, that is, what is the motivation for the appraisal: personal interest, utility to an outside professional or agency, benefit to the self-helpers or another external purpose such as contribution to research based elsewhere?

Permutations of evaluators may be devised from three basic options: an external specialist evaluator not employed by the self-helpers or the relevant professional agency, an internal specialist evaluator employed directly by the agency and/or self-helpers, or self-helpers and/or involved social workers themselves.

Key *et al.* (1976, p. 25–7) summarises the issues raised by the choice of evaluator. On the whole, the more 'inside' a person is, the more acceptable to peers, the cheaper the appraisal and the closer to the intimacies of what is happening. But perhaps in such cases the evaluator is more hamstrung when it comes to presenting a fearlessly critical and objective account. On the other hand, the further 'outside' the evaluator stands, the more the claim of objective distance will have to be balanced against the time spent getting close to the complex heart of things. Objectivity also may be claimed, but no more achieved, by the outsider than by the insider.

Finally, Patton (1982, p. 223) notes that the whole debate should not be presented, as it often is, in terms of alternatives, since in practice many effective appraisals have been carried out by combinations of insiders and outsiders working together.

Process studies

In many ways, process studies are incompatible with evaluative research since they tend to concentrate on the process of a group, scheme, project or organisation and/or the nature of the experience of involvement from the standpoint of participants. To this extent they may be descriptive and involve qualitative methods of data collection, with particular regard to the way members experience being in a group. It is often said that experience expresses its own inherent validity in the uniqueness of its subjective quality. Advocates of this view may argue that process research invalidates externally based appraisal.

Yet it is important to recognise that this polarisation between process and outcome studies is somewhat artificial. It is not necessary for intuitive reflection of group processes to obliterate rational appraisal of group outcomes. The two may be regarded as complementary. In a study of twenty various self-help groups, Levy found that they were dealing not only with their members' problems but also with their most fundamental human needs such as 'for empathetic understanding, for enhanced self-esteem, for meaning, and for an opportunity to express their feelings and share their experiences with another' (Levy, 1979, p. 271). He suggests this may explain why most members would expect to stay indefinitely in their groups.

Studying involvement　In one respect, process studies contribute invaluable insights to evaluative research. The context in which the effectiveness of a self-help group is evaluated tends to be as transient as the lives of many groups themselves. Clearly, self-help activities are not often as long-lived as organisations and institutions such as social work teams, hospitals or resource bases.

Having said that, members of some self-help organisations are likely to feel justifiably proud, not so much of the speed with which they gained control of their problems, but of the number of years they have been members of a group or organisation. Membership is too unspecific a term to apply to the multitude of levels of attendance, involvement and intensity which is possible in a self-help programme. One member may attend every meeting for years but remain relatively invisible in the group, while another attends occasionally but is always noticeable. The sporadic attendance of a third over a long period may correspond with intermittent stresses in everyday life. Again, it is worth considering the kind of organisation which involves a postal network. How does one set out to assess the outcome in such circumstances?

Studying membership succession　A further complication arises when one considers that many groups and organisations attract successions of members in view of their open-ended character. The term 'serial reciprocity' has been used (Richardson and Goodman, 1983, p. 96) to describe the pattern of involvement by means of which members feed back into groups some form of support after they themselves have been helped. This seems to be one of the most effective ways in which members can contribute to group life. We can anticipate also that over a period, different members will be at different stages in the process. However, patterns of participation differ according to the nature of the focus which draws people together. It has been observed that those caring for relatives of people with learning disabilities tend to remain long-term members of self-help groups, in contrast with the generally brief membership of widows and single parents (Richardson and Goodman, 1983, p. 97).

In this connection, it helps if sufficient 'senior' members are present in an open-ended group to give stability and continuity, without it becoming so top heavy that new, potential members are discouraged from joining. It may be helpful also for members to feel that they are all at the same stage of discussing and coming to terms with their problems (Richardson and Goodman, 1983, p. 98) and this may even militate against open-ended groups.

So before and after measurement or testing, even if self-helpers allowed it, would not necessarily illuminate the quality of the experience of self-help. Neither would it identify events in the lives of group members, such as accidents, traumas or one-off incidents.

Studying group processes   This approach often makes more sense than looking for outcomes, especially in relatively long-term or open-ended groups, projects or schemes.

Outcome studies

Appraisal may take a number of forms: individual outcome, comparative outcome, impact on the group or the community. It is possible to view the outcome from the standpoint of any of the parties to the activity and this may include the participants, whether professional or lay, other people outside the direct experience of the activity, such as relatives, or some other organisation or group. In such studies, there is no guarantee of a consensus between these vantage points. The community at large may want the consumer to behave quietly, the professional may desire for the consumer some kind of ultimate cure from a problem or condition, while the consumer simply may want to feel relief in the here and now.

Traditionally, psychologists undertaking outcome appraisal may have looked in the direction of *attitude change* in the individual. The impact of an activity upon an individual may depend on what sorts of significant change is brought about. Indeed, some would question the extent to which people's attitudes, let alone their personalities, are amenable to such changes. Another way of formulating the task involves focussing on the problem rather than on the person. However, this requires that the problem itself can be defined in terms which permit appraisal.

Answers to the following questions need to be found. How is the problem specified? How will changes in its character and intensity be measured? How can we be sure that such changes are the direct consequences of self-help activity and do not proceed from other as yet unconsidered factors? (Lieberman and Bond, 1978, p. 225). The difficulty of research in this area is that 'prepost' measurement is difficult or impossible since a person is likely to become involved in an activity after the problem becomes difficult to handle. So the appraisal cannot reach back to examine the individual in her or his circumstances before involvement commenced (Lieberman and Borman, 1976, p. 460). Whether the research is concerned with the group member or the problem, the criteria for judging effectiveness are equally important. These depend both on the way effectiveness is conceptualised and also on the theoretical perspective of the person evaluating.

At what time will it be done?

Does the appraisal have to be completed yesterday (a common requirement in bureaucracies), in the near future, or at some indeterminate date?

Such questions begin to shape the timing of data collection. Commonly, some form of appraisal will be called for in any activity where there is an element of statutory funding. It may even be built into some regular process of review. In these circumstances, it is useful to develop guidelines for review and to ensure that the appraisal is compatible with them.

Over what period will it be done?

Will the appraisal be carried out over a short term, say two weeks, or over a long period, such as five years? Whereas much appraisal is, as they say, quick and dirty, sometimes self-helpers and/or social workers may be able to justify to themselves, and possibly even to a funding person or other source, the idea of carrying out fairly lengthy study of the issues raised during the life of an activity. The disadvantage of this may be that the data and results will possess all those features of qualitative, open-ended research which irritate hard-nosed seekers after evaluative proof. The advantages include the possible ongoing interaction between insights gained about the processes of the activity and the constant refining and re-conceptualisation which is stimulated in the research process itself. As was noted at the outset of this chapter, much appraisal involves continually going back and reformulating both the questions needing answering and the method of answering them.

Carrying out the appraisal   There are three main stages involved in the appraisal process: reflection, programming and doing the job, each of which involves particular tasks. We deal with producing and using the appraisal separately below.

Reflection

This begins before the appraisal has started and continues throughout. In settings where the activities change direction and character, or where qualitative methodology is used, the person doing the appraisal needs to be accustomed constantly to putting the entire research act under scrutiny and being prepared to shift objectives, change the emphasis and area of data collection, rethink the analysis and projected outcomes. At the more bread-and-butter level, the process of reflection needs to focus on the data gathered.

Programming

There generally is a point when those involved in the appraisal feel able to make some practical plans and draw up some kind of programme. In the light of the previous paragraph, it is clear that while this needs to be firm enough to enable effective progress to be made, it should be sufficiently flexible to cope with necessary changes.

Doing the job

This stage involves translating the programme into action and making sure some kind of limits are set to the study. This latter point is important because there is a great temptation to devise research which is too grand ever to be achieved. The task needs to be kept manageable.

To this end, it is very important to set some realistic *deadlines* for each stage of the process, and to stick to them.

The procedure of carrying out a quantitative study may make it possible to separate out these stages fairly clearly. But in qualitative research, there is usually no clear point at which the collection of evidence ceases and the analysis begins. Often what happens is that the process of analysis begins as soon as the evaluator starts to pick over the evidence and draw some preliminary conclusions, to be fed back into further attempts to gather evidence. This process is pretty well circular and may go on right to the end of the study. In the final phase, there is always the need to consider what will happen if the outcome of the research is not a happy ending.

For instance, appraisal of women's consciousness-raising groups has highlighted the divergence between them and other helping groups, in respect of their impact on women's problems. A striking contrast exists between the symptom reduction achieved in psychotherapy and the lack of impact of consciousness-raising groups on people's symptoms. Rather than the emphasis in consciousness-raising groups being upon personal growth or change, it is evident in increased self-esteem and the recognition of self-worth (Howell, 1981, p. 595).

Producing and using the appraisal

If all has gone reasonably well, though not necessarily according to plan as we have seen above, there will be something to report back to others. This is an important stage. Far too often, the results of research stay in someone's filing cabinet as 'that brilliant study I will write up some day when there is time'. Provided the above cautions have been heeded, the scope of the study is kept modest and the deadlines have been adhered to, the main skill required now is the assertiveness actually to commit oneself to sharing the results with others, either in written form or by face to face meetings with them. How it is done does not matter as much as ensuring that it happens!

The usefulness of appraisal: a caution

The key question here from the vantage point of the evaluator is how relevant, reliable, comprehensive or systematic the evidence is. This depends on how successfully the above questions have been addressed.

From the vantage point of the person involved in self-help, the key question may be whether or not the appraisal is going to contribute to the future life of the activity, or sabotage it. From the viewpoint of rigorous research, effective appraisal depends on the evaluator satisfying a number of important criteria, including reliability, validity, comparability with other appraisals and relevance to the population being evaluated. Self-help activities are just as prone to all the problems raised by trying to meet these criteria as any other aspect of social work.

On the whole, there is little indication from research that self-help can be proved to benefit participants. But that does not appear to prevent people taking part and appearing to gain a good deal from activities. Within the broad field of self-help more attention has been paid to tackling the appraisal of groupwork than anything else. In this respect, the lack of proof of outcome effectiveness does not contrast particularly with other aspects of groupwork. For example, the popularity of sensitivity-oriented groups has not been lessened by the general lack of research indicating that they have any beneficial results (Back, 1972, p. 14).

From the standpoint of self-helpers, it is necessary to bear in mind the likelihood that rigorous appraisal will suggest that not all the outcomes of self-help will be positive. After all, there is evidence to this effect. Consciousness-raising groups may have adverse effects on members. Howell (1981, p. 596) records the sabotage of a group, which disbanded rather than face threats from a suicidal woman. Nor apparently, is consciousness-raising any substitute for the psychotherapy from which a neurotic person may benefit (Howell, 1981, p. 598). Further, some individuals may break down in psychoses or experience a range of less serious but significant traumas including the loss of their defences, with no substitute being provided (Back, 1972, p. 221). Women's consciousness-raising groups in the feminist movement offer a distinctive history, relying on persuasion to maintain a political feminist ideology and avoid groups becoming therapeutic (Bond and Reibstein, 1979).

There is evidence that women joining consciousness-raising groups use psychotherapy more than the general population and that their motives for joining are not significantly associated with dissatisfaction with existing services (Lieberman, 1979, pp. 150–63). In the case of widows' groups, far from members coming together through dissatisfaction with inadequate professional services, groups possibly serve the function of remedying failed social networks and do not serve a population coterminus with the client groups of professionals (Bankoff, 1979, pp. 192–3). In an evaluative study of fifteen women's consciousness-raising groups, Lieberman *et al.* (1979, pp. 356–61) found that most seemed to have a limited though useful therapeutic value and did not reduce the problems of women or encourage personal growth like encounter groups. On the other hand, women gained an enhanced perspective on their circumstances. The researchers conclude that consciousness-raising is no substitute for therapy for women with chronic or severe problems and did not change their lifestyles, but it enabled the mildly depressed to revise and improve their self-image.

Evidence from other areas of self-help corroborates this view that it may not be fruitful to judge the outcome of group activities in simple terms such as problem reduction. In an appraisal of the impact of a medical self-help group, Videka (1979, p. 386) found that its value was in helping people manage their problems and maintain their sense of self-worth rather than in reforming them or encouraging introspection or interpersonal learning. In general, then, there is no proof that self-help activities will benefit participants. On the contrary, there are indications that some people experiencing some kinds of groups may be harmed.

Possible products of appraisal

Will the outcome of appraisal be simply used for personal reflection? Will it lead to the sharing of experiences simply between participants in the self-help activity? Will some form of written report be written, summarising the findings of the appraisal? For which audience will it be written? Will the appraisal be used by professionals, self-helpers, students or the general reader?

Will the product be a formal summary of survey findings or questionnaire results, or a case study in the form of pen-pictures? To what extent will the product be tailored to the requirements of some external demand, such as the need to justify continued funding? Will this mean that the product is more of a public relations exercise than an objective, critical study?

The reality is that the needs of most activities are likely to be met best by a series of different sorts of products at different times for different purposes and audiences. A plan based on that tactic would seem more attainable than the idea of a single mammoth work, produced years after everybody has long gone who was connected with the activity (or, more likely by that stage, perpetually in a state of revision and never finally published at all).

The most appropriate point to leave the appraisal is at the point where the social worker is considering, in the same careful way as at the outset, how to *feed back the findings*. The process of this needs to involve self-helpers as centrally as it did when the preparations for the appraisal were being made. Absolutely central to this process, of course, is the issue of who owns the appraisal document, what control the self-helpers have over its contents, and what their power is to negotiate changes in it, or even to veto statements with which they may disagree. Finally, what provision is there for the self-helpers to contribute their own comments to the appraisal? This is moment of truth, in which the power relationships between participants in a self-help activity may be laid bare.

Summary

In Chapter 7, we have reviewed a number of questions and issues, each of which is crucial to effective appraisal of self-help activity. This has been done in the sequence of four major stages which the practitioner undertaking appraisal will need to consider. In conclusion, here is a checklist of the main stages and within each, some key questions and issues which need to be considered:

The Process of Appraisal

Clarifying the task

- Whom will this appraisal empower?
- Who controls the appraisal?
- What sort of appraisal is sought?
- Critical Appraisal: A case study approach preferred
- What is being appraised?

Preparing for the appraisal

- Collecting information
- Sources of information
- What evidence will be collected?
- Problems of information gathering
- Process and outcome studies
- At what time will it be done?
- Over what period will it be done?

Carrying out the appraisal

- Reflection
- Programming
- Doing the job.

Producing and using the appraisal

- Possible products of the appraisal.

8

Self-Helpers and Social Workers

Chapter 8 examines the relationship between social workers and those involved in self-help activities, looking first at some of the cautions and subsequently at some pointers towards effective relationships between them.

Cautions

In this first part of the chapter, we summarise the four major areas of risk to the activities of both self-helpers and professionals, posed by self-help: namely, the inherently problematic relationship between professionals and self-helpers, ways in which each party may retreat from, or corrupt the challenge thereby posed and finally the difficulties of handling the element of power in the relationship.

Self-helpers and social workers: a problematic relationship

Once the consent of the consumer of social services to the way she or he is dealt with can no longer be taken for granted, then the so-called 'proper' relationship between the social worker and the client becomes problematic. Or rather, it was always problematic only we acknowledge now that it cannot be ignored. In any case, there has been evidence for some time that, clients apart, social workers have not even developed relationships with non-professional helpers to their full potential (Holme and Maizels,

1978). Further, it may be that the worker will tend to hold clients responsible in one way or another for this state of affairs, things are 'not what they used to be' in the agency. Social workers are not treated with respect 'like they were in the old days'. They are less likely to be thanked by their clients than attacked, verbally through criticism or even beaten up. Consumers of social work, too, may accuse social workers of causing some sort of deterioration in relations between receiver and deliverer of services.

In short, in contemporary social work consumers are increasingly likely to question such autonomy and authority as the practitioner possesses (Haug and Sussman, 1969, p. 154). These days, the mistakes of social workers and the areas of their practice which may be less than ideal are more and more likely to be the subjects of critical scrutiny, not only by clients but by other professionals, the media and the general public.

Resistance by consumers to the exercise of power by social workers may be passive. They may opt out or refuse to co-operate. Or it may be active, in which case they may petition, sit-in, strike, riot or contact a lawyer. Consumers may also doubt that social workers have the requisite knowledge to deal with them effectively and may claim the right to define the problem and subsequently to determine not to call upon the social worker but simply to try and manage their own problems.

If we locate the postwar popularity of self-help groups in the context of such disillusionment with social services on the part of the consumer, then the character of the self-help movement takes on a critical dimension. Far from our being able to dismiss self-help largely as the middle-class playing at alternative therapies or as a reactionary shift away from State support and towards self-support it emerges, in part at least, as a sign of the consumer revolt against some forms of social work.

So we need to treat with caution any indications that social workers are negotiating with the self-help field. The issue is not whether they are being useful, but whether they are colonising, invading, or inappropriately interfering. In dealing with it, such contemporary fashions as new careerism, aides, lay helpers, volunteers as well as professional facilitators need to be examined.

Consumer control: a false promise?   In the light of the examination in Chapters 3–5 of three typical attempts to blur the distinction between professional and client, we need now to locate the dynamic between the worker and the consumer of social work in its organisational context. At first sight, Dumont's exposition of the 'new face of professionalism' (Dumont, 1972) complements the growing popularity of self-help in social work and offers optimism about the capacity of governments and agencies for social change. Dumont identifies six principles in the new face of professionalism: consumer control, indifference to credentials, a sense of common language and purpose transcending individual professional practice, a critical attitude, impatience with the pace of change, and an investment in political activity.

'Meta-professionalism' The last three of these principles are unexceptionable to many professionals and the third – what amounts to meta-professionalism – has been around in social work in Britain, in Intermediate Treatment for instance (Adams, 1976), for many years. But it can be argued first that the extent of the new professionalism is exaggerated by Dumont and that it is restricted to students and the influential as well as members of some reforming movements; second that its influence is likely to be limited; third that if the new professionalism implies that professionals should not claim exclusive rights over any distinctive knowledge and skills, then this is a spurious argument for non-professionalism.

Retreat by professionals from the challenge

Three forms of retreat are likely: that self-help contributes to the reinforcement of professional complacency, that professional agencies opt out, or that self-helpers retreat into alternativism.

Reinforcing professional complacency While self-help groups could be dismissed as having no discernable impact on the consumer group served by existing statutory services, at the same time this is too simple and inaccurate a denunciation. It is true that some groups may actually support the political status quo and that if any seriously threaten to invade the territorial powerbase of professional activities, in local authorities at any rate, there might be some significant legal battles (Robinson and Henry, 1977, p. 136). But there are some striking examples of self-help activities impinging on those statutory services without themselves coming under threat. Perhaps the activities we have described as autonomous in Chapter 5 are safest in this respect.

The reality is that the threat to the quality of helping services and activities is more insidious. In the health field, it has been observed that most self-help groups hold the same view of health and illness as do more conventional helpers (Robinson and Henry, 1977, p. 126). In the activities they studied, Robinson and Henry found that the focus is upon helping individual people with problems rather than upon the broader structural features of the situation in which they live, such as the problems of homelessness, overcrowding, loneliness, stress, and so on. In such circumstances, self-help activities actually may make more pronounced the very health problems they seek to alleviate (Robinson and Henry, 1977, p. 126), by meeting immediate needs, deluding people into thinking that local action will solve their problems, diverting people from seeking their proper share of potential services and giving officials and agencies an excuse to neglect the provision that is due to people.

A further consequence may be to exacerbate a split between caring and technical aspects of medical practice. Using the example of the Cancer Aftercare and Rehabilitation Society (CARE), Robinson and Henry suggest that because the cancer patient is given regular medical checks, the work of CARE begins by picking up the emotional needs of the patient. Self-help groups may thus simply follow on and reinforce the existing direction of professional practice, in the less technical and challenging or critical areas (Robinson and Henry, 1977, p. 128). But as the authors acknowledge, reducing the scope of professional activities to the technical area could be seen as positive, in that in the process their power is circumscribed and to a degree limited.

Opting out by agencies Co-operation in the form of working partnerships between paid social workers and volunteers, or interweaving of statutory and voluntary services, may be welcomed in principle. But care needs to be taken that self-help is not seen as a way of cutting costs by the erosion of statutory services (Darvill and Munday, 1984, p. 5). The paid worker and the volunteer both have distinctive contributions to make to services and each may enrich what the other provides. The greater the tendency for government to argue for retrenchment in the responsibility of the state for people's welfare, the more there is a risk that budget cuts will be made progressively and more swiftly in areas of work where people seem to be developing self-help competences. This presents professionals with the need to work out strategies for defending the self-help field against negative consequences of its very successes, and ensuring the appropriate measures are taken by agency providers to defend resources.

Alternativism: danger or opportunity?   The rationales for self-help seem to imply that it flourishes when disenchantment with existing services and associated supporting organisations and networks is running high. But more than that, self-help activity may be infused with the distinct but often connected strains of alternativism or even anti-professionalism. This is not to deny that many professionals themselves may allow, facilitate, encourage, participate in or even stimulate self-help activities. But often the enthusiasm for an activity runs side by side with antagonism towards an individualistic, privatised, competitive social environment. We can predict that in general terms integral activities will be less likely to take an anti-professional stance than autonomous ones. In general, it seems likely that the more radical the activity the more tenuous and potentially conflict-ridden its links with professional workers will be.

There is nothing intrinsically wrong with adopting an anti-professional stance. But the consequence of standing off from contact with professionals may be a retreat into alternative activity rather than maintaining a constant debate with the professional world and continually challenging existing practice. The problem with self-help may be that to the extent that professionals are able to dismiss it as merely another alternative, it may lose its power to act as a critique of what social workers, health visitors, doctors and nurses do. Those who retreat to an alternative position should not be criticised for it. It could be that professionals have treated them perfunctorily once too often, which is a pity when it happens. Social workers ignore criticism from consumers at their peril.

Corruption by professionals of the challenge

The relationship between social workers and self-helpers is vulnerable to corruption from three directions: the exploitation, the professionalisation or the co-option of self-helpers as non-professionals.

Exploitation of non-professional helpers There is a risk also that self-helpers may be seen just as another kind of volunteer. At the start of this chapter, we noted how the potential benefits of volunteers have not been realised by social workers. On the whole, in Britain, it seems as though the main role of helpers of professional social workers has been in befriending and practical services, while in the probation service they have been involved in befriending and counselling (Holme and Maizels, 1978, p. 88). Experience in New York of using indigenous non-professionals as aides in mental health has served the function of providing psychological first aid and acting as a means of intervention in community health issues. Aides may thus improve service delivery and help to increase the understanding of mental health problems held by more traditional staff. In addition to providing direct services, community action and community education, it is suggested that aides may also take on the role of social planners (Hallowitz and Riessman, 1967). But these are suggestions only, in a world where non-professional helping plays a very restricted part in many professionals' working week.

The use of non-professionals should not be undertaken lightly. Here the word 'use' acquires significance in itself. In the New York example quoted above, some aides feared exploitation and felt relatively ignorant of basic skills such as routine recording, as well as feeling they were rivals with professionals. In this sense, Hallowitz's aides remain inescapably subservient, secondary in importance and dependent on the professionals.

Knight and Hayes advocate the use of non-professional or indigenous workers, in the light of limited but encouraging research, indicating that 'non-professional or indigenous workers have a number of advantages over professionals. Living in the same neighbourhood, they do not commute, and have a knowledge of their locality that can only come from living there. They are of the same social class as those they are trying to help, do not have narrowly defined professional roles, and can offer friendship rather than just a service, they are less threatening to local people because they do not have elements of control or power, or the association with the state, that workers in official social work agencies have' (1981, p. 96). They admit that indigenous workers do tend to take on too much work and risk burning out, but that proper professional support can alleviate this.

Professionalisation of self-helpers   Self-help activities may be prone to the insidious process of professionalising the participants. To understand this, we need to distinguish between the kind of wisdom acquired by professionals and the experiential wisdom gained by members of self-help groups. At the point when members achieve control over their own problems they are in a position to manage aspects of their own lives independently from the practice of professionals. But, in the context of health groups, it has been observed that many self-help groups fail to capitalise on this opportunity. They do not work out the implications of the power they possess. The consequence is that group members give themselves help which does not differ significantly from that offered them by professionals. The only difference is that they are administering it themselves (Robinson and Henry, 1977, p. 129).

Co-option by professionals   The biggest threat to self-help is of a take-over by professional practice. Take-overs are not just a danger in business, but may occur in any setting where the power of one group over a market is affected by the existence of successful competitors. The more effective self-help activities become, the more they are at risk of co-option by professionals. Self-appointed experts, media personalities, researchers, writers and practitioners in many fields appear from time to time, riding on the backs of self-helpers. Professionals can make only a limited contribution to self-help endeavours before they begin to take over and reduce other people's belief in their ability to break out of constraints and take control of their own circumstances.

But in spite of these risks, there is room for optimism, especially in the case of the more resilient self-help activity. Marieskind's observation on women's groups probably has a wider relevance:

> Despite the vulnerability to co-option, the self-help group is an invaluable concept. It is not just a personal solution for individual women's needs – although that alone is a valid reason for its existence. The self-help group is a tool for inducing collective thought and action, and radical social change (Marieskind, 1984, pp. 31–2).

The gains accruing from collaboration between professionals and self-helpers may be counter-balanced by the potential dangers. Self-helpers may gain credibility, support and resources from professional help, but may sacrifice independence. Kleiman *et al.* (1976) records some of the hazards of partnerships between self-help and professionals. In the American Cancer Society project examined by Kleiman, professionals tended to criticise helpers for their lack of such as counselling skills and volunteers did not have the motivation and assertiveness to take charge of the running of the project themselves. Kleiman concludes depressingly:

> Can a self-help group find happiness within an agency? We must answer that it cannot. The growing popularity of this approach leads to hasty attempts to transplant a few features of self-help groups to the alien environment of agency setting. Inevitably the arbitrary extraction of self-help principles from the nurturant and supportive milieu of the group invites failure: the auto-immune systems of the host agency work to reject the graft. The bureaucratic directives and structural constraints imposed by agencies contravene the entire purpose and meaning of self-help – *leadership from below* (Kleiman *et al.*, 1976, p. 409, emphasis in original).

It is difficult to predict the outcome of challenges by clients to professional knowledge and power. It is very unlikely that they will lead to the total dismantling of such professional autonomy as social workers possess and more likely that the consequence will be 'a narrowing of professional authority to the most limited and esoteric elements of his knowledge base' (Haug and Sussman, 1969, p. 159). Self-help activity is capable of growing through the redefinition of this uncertain territory between professionals and clients.

The problems of power

Having seen repeatedly in Chapters 3–5 how significant is the element of power in the relationship between social workers and non-professional self-helpers, we identify here four specific dangers; playing power games, toning down of the intensity of the self-help experience, fragmentation of non-professional interests, and threats to social workers by expert self-helpers.

Playing power games to avoid empowering self-helpers　Is the power imbalance between professionals and self-helpers immune to pressure from the consumer to democratise? There is a risk that tokenistic activity by professionals may result merely in formal nodding to principles such as consumer participation. It is significant that behind many debates about the relations between providers and consumers of social services lies the issue of *power*. Self-help tends to espouse the principle of power sharing between professional and lay helpers. This is familiar to social workers, many of whom accept as normal the principles of openness of communication with, and accessibility to, clients and even a devolution of skills to clients and self-helpers in areas formerly regarded as a professional monopoly. It is in this light that a recent commentator could say that 'unconditional regard for another is not a skill or property of a professionally trained person. Stupid lovers can demonstrate it . . . and it can be demonstrated by group members for each other' (Hurvitz, 1974, p. 106).

The ultimate demystification involves encouraging self-helpers that helping skills can be acquired like other skills, and we saw in Chapter 6 that this is a prominent element in the self-help literature in Britain.

Toning down the intensity of the self-help experience　Advocacy can be fudged and self-advocacy may remain a gleam in the eye. Self-help may be implemented in a tokenistic fashion, the anger of consumers or their dissatisfaction with existing services defused through protracted negotiation or some other bureaucratic process. The critical perspective of consumers on the services with which they have been in contact may have been blunted in the process.

The anger of self-helpers may be translated into respectable language, their style proceduralised and their language sanitised. Professionals may play a part, deliberately or unwittingly, in socialising them in the proper procedures for gaining access to resources and skills which will empower them.

In all this, there is the constant danger that self-help will run out of steam and function like the professional service. In consequence, self-helpers lose the chance to share in management.

Admittedly, this may not be the fault solely of the professionals. Within the self-helpers' camp there may be factions. Some may want to ape professional practice without appreciating that others prefer to plough the more difficult but for them fertile furrow of consumerism. Among self-helpers, too, the assertive may advocate for others, removing their scope for self-advocacy. There is no reason why among self-helpers there should be any more homogeneity of beliefs than exists among professionals.

Fragmentation of non-professional interests   When we compare the circumstances of workers in agencies with those of clients or consumers, it is easy to see that in areas such as the health and social services the professional workers are a concentrated interest with plenty of continuity built into their relatively powerful position. In contrast, most clients are in a dispersed situation. They have relatively slight chances of meeting to develop a common approach to negotiating handling with or by their professionals. How often do groups of people meet to compare notes on their visits to the same out-patients' clinic, general practitioners' surgery or social services office? It is hard to consider how we would set about the logistic task of organising this, let alone how we would persuade professionals and consumers alike of its desirability.

A consequence of the way helping services are organised and delivered is that each self-help enterprise tends to get on in isolation from others, unless it is affiliated to a common organisational base. In the health field, this tendency for people to get on with the running of their own activities has been noted, along with the consequence that far from different self-help groups joining forces to deal with common problems, they are more often than not fragmented by divergencies of local beliefs and practice, competitiveness and petty squabbles (Robinson and Henry, 1977, p. 130).

Threats to social workers by expert self-helpers   From the viewpoint of hard-pressed social workers, insecure about their professional credibility, there may be conflict between enjoying the superior status and omniscience invested in them by having non-professional self-helpers working alongside them, together with the anxiety that this cannot be lived up to. There is also the potential conflict between keenness to see non-professionals develop skills and reluctance to hand over to them responsibility and autonomy and anxiety that non-professionals, however unwitting-ly, will do damage.

It is possible also that relationships between professionals and self-helpers highlight the threat posed by the more active and immediate response of the expert lay practitioner to client need, in contrast with the more deliberately assessed and planned course of the professional's intervention. It is also probable, of course, that the self-helping non-professional has more time to do a thorough job of supporting a fellow member of a self-help group than a hard-pressed social worker. There is no doubt that the informal practices of many a self-help group reinforce spontaneity and informality and pose a threat to the professional, who relies on traditional communications and lines of authority. There is a sense in which this caricatures, but it illustrates the potential difficulties of bridging the gap between the professional's traditional methods and style and those of the self-helper. Naturally, when the association between self-helper and social worker works it brings advantages, such as the enthusiasm and conviction self-helpers bring to their activities and the encouragement they may give to professionals to experiment with new methods.

Effective relationships between self-helpers and social workers

In the second part of this chapter, a number of general principles are advanced, as the foundation for a healthy relationship between social work and self-help activities in a locality.

Empowerment should be mutual

Essentially, the ideal relationship between social workers and self-helpers would be one in which each witnessed, and possibly contributed actively towards, the empowerment of the other. This is far easier to set down on paper than it is to achieve in practice.

Optimism should be cultivated

In a survey of the views of mental health professionals about self-help groups, Levy (1976, p. 311) found that whilst over 46 per cent thought self-help groups had an important part to play in a comprehensive mental health service, less than a third saw it as likely that their agency would be interested in integrating self-help activities with the services they provided. However, the findings of Levy's survey confirms the view of Lieberman and Borman that on the whole self-help activities are viewed by self-helpers as complementary with, rather than antagonistic towards, professionals (Levy, 1982, p. 1273).

The desired relationship between professionals and self-helpers is defined fundamentally by whether the self-helpers view their activity as integral, facilitated or autonomous in relation to professionals. If the latter, then there is little more to be said, since they will not want professionals involved in their activities, and this stance must be respected by professional workers themselves. However, in the case of integral or facilitated activities, self-helpers and professionals may each gain from contact and Judy Wilson (1986, pp. 84–95) points out many of these benefits. For self-helpers they include resources such as meeting places, administrative help and transport, publicity, extra help through students, credibility through use of an agency address. For professionals the gains may be increased knowledge about the needs of self-helpers and the chance to improve services thereby.

Non-compromising professional support

Undoubtedly there is a need for self-help activities to retain a degree of autonomy appropriate to their circumstances. While they may benefit from learning how to build effective links with existing professional services, it is not in their interest to be taken over and incorporated into such services. As a consequence they could lose their independent identity and much of their creative enthusiasm (Tyler, 1976, p. 447). Relations between self-helpers and professionals should be seen as tender and nurtured accordingly. In Liz Evans's study of self-help groups of parents of children with disabilities, she found that professionals could react defensively when parents started becoming enthusiastic and assertive about care. In fact, suspicion tended to be mutual. Whilst newsletters from carers to professionals helped to inform them about what was happening, in the two groups where problems did not arise several factors may have contributed: first, the fact that groups already existed in their areas and had prepared professionals to be more accepting, second, the existence of co-ordinated leadership by groups with experience and third, the greater care taken in preparation for joint meetings between parents and professionals (Evans *et al.*, 1986, p. 43).

Clarifying the basis of work between social workers and self-helpers

We can build on Phyllida Parsloe's extremely useful paper (Parsloe, 1986, p. 13) in which she identifies three social work skills: ensuring clients understand the political as well as the personal nature of their problems, that this is communicated adequately to managers, councillors and the public at large, and that the level of social services are defended. This leads to what Parsloe calls a 'professional anti-professional' approach (Parsloe, 1986, p. 14), which includes seeing clients as departmental resources in the context of creating open sharing relationships with them and advocating both for them and on behalf of the personal social services. In pursuit of this, there is a reciprocal need for social policy to support self-help efforts, through legislation. Consultative personnel and skills should also be made available, as well as the willingness to liaise with and facilitate activity without threatening to take it over.

Sol Tax (Tax, 1976, p. 450) argues that if traditional primary groups like the family, church and neighbourhood were given more support there would not be such a vacuum left by the withering of these, for the new self-help groups to fill. Tax is less sure about the value of organising self-help in, say, a Bureau of Self-Help Groups Affairs, since self-help should begin with a level of awareness in the community itself which simply encourages groups to develop as they wish. Whatever we feel about Tax's value judgement concerning the vulnerability of primary groups in the modern world, it is undeniable that people involved in self-help which relates in one way or another to professional activities should have access to appropriate sources of support, resources, consultation and so on, without in the process having to compromise essential elements of their position in the self-help field.

In effect, the clarification of this relationship between professional workers and self-helpers should enable the social worker to sort out more rigorously and effectively the distinctive roles which need to be adopted in integral, facilitated and autonomous settings, ensuring in the process the preservation of the integrity of what the self-helpers are doing.

Real empowerment

Quite simply, social workers should beware of the tendency to delegate rather than to hand over real power. The acid test is the willingness to give self-helpers the actual resources to do the job themselves. In this area, tokenism is to be deplored.

Opportunities of localism

To be effective, self-help needs to be a collaboration with professionals which recognises the distinctive contribution which self-helpers can make.

Tony Gibson's thesis is that small-scale, local grassroots action groups are an antidote to the bureaucratic strangulation which afflicts our centralised society (Gibson, 1979, p. 15). He argues that, contrary to popular belief, ordinary people, without skills, special training or even the confidence to do it, can take a lead and run these self-help community action groups (Gibson, 1979, p. 17). He points out that in the process the relationship between professionals and lay people may need to be redefined in favour of the latter (Gibson, 1979, p. 128). Perhaps a degree of training, support and resources to underpin such activity should be negotiated where possible, though, from social work agencies.

Community-based methods of organisation

It is accepted that there is a need not to fixate on the notion of community and patch as panaceas for practice. However, some extremely useful principles can be itemised as a basis for more detailed development in the light of local circumstances. Drawing on a BASW paper (BASW, 1984, p. 14). Roger Hadley's recent book (Hadley *et al.*, 1987) and some recent work by Gawlinski (Gawlinski, 1988), we can assert the need for social workers to respect the client perspective in all their work and build up their understanding of local networks and relationships. Additionally, it is important to try to achieve a broad concept of teamwork, including in the team a greater mix of people, such as aides, volunteers and consumers. Clearly, in the light of Chapters 4 and 5 in particular, social workers engaging with self-help should avoid the temptation to incorporate self-helpers wholesale into the professional framework of activity. In other words, the typology of self-help activity we have put forward here enables our notions of teamwork to become increasingly complex and sophisticated.

Whether or not the patch approach is taken as appropriate, there is a general need for social workers to support and maintain the strength of other professional services, voluntary agencies and the informal sector in their locality, rather than either undermining them or handing over to them tasks whilst withdrawing from the responsibilities of adequately resourcing them. Bamford identifies seven useful principles inherent in Hadley and McGrath's (1980) approach to community-based social work:

- Locally based team focusing on small areas or patches
- The capacity to obtain detailed information about the patch
- Accessibility and acceptability to the patch population
- Close liaison with other local agencies and groups
- Integration of all field and domiciliary services within patch teams
- Participative management
- Substantial autonomy exercised by patch teams (Bamford, 1982, p. 96).

Building onto the statutory, informal and voluntary sectors

It has been argued that the relationship between self-help groups, as part of the informal sector of social care, and the voluntary sector should be symbiotic (Wolfenden, 1978, p. 28). The voluntary sector generally offers a less bureaucratic and a more flexible means of support and encouragement than do many agencies in the statutory sector. Some self-help activities which lack any other formal organisational connections or reference points of their own, will welcome the support offered by a voluntary body and may even prefer it to a link with a statutory agency.

This involves the informal as well as the voluntary sectors. Self-help in the area of work with elderly people, for example, involves relatives and carers as well as elderly people themselves. More often than not, it is the carers who initiate self-help schemes to meet their own needs for self-care. At this juncture, the process of helping elderly people is furthered by networks of individuals, groups and organisations which exemplify the inter-connectedness of formal and informal patterns of caring in the community. An obvious area for self-help to develop is in the support of those who care for confused elderly relatives. On one hand, this may be viewed positively as enriching sources of support in the informal sector. Alternatively, it may be seen as one consequence of public policy leaving many carers for the elderly unsupported at home, looking after them.

It could be said that although agencies have responsibility for providing social services, often the burden of quality control, that is, ensuring that the service to the consumer *feels* adequate, rests on consumers themselves. In this sense, while the responsibility for services may rest with management in the organisation, the task of verifying good social work experiences is left with the client. But social workers should not accept this state of affairs complacently. Bamford has identified their responsibilities, arguing that the role of social services is 'that of supporting voluntary care, of providing direct care for those who need it, and of recognising the importance of breaking down barriers between the community and the professionals. Translating these concepts into practice requires a radical shift in professional attitudes' (Bamford, 1982, p. 96).

Profane practice

If professional services exemplify the sacred principles of practice, then self-help perhaps needs to express something profane. It is unfortunate that we have to make the point in this fashion, rather than in reverse, since self-help should be capable of acting as the reciprocal to whatever services exist, rather than simply as a radical alternative.

Progress in this area depends on the ability of social workers to avoid the risk their clients will slide further into poverty and isolation. We can argue with Balloch that people need jobs and relief from poverty and isolation rather than self-help and exhortations to help themselves (Balloch, 1985, pp. 105–6). However, it is necessary to reach beyond the vague exhortation to practitioners to engage in action to improve the social environment in which their clients live. Phyllida Parsloe argues that social work should avoid escaping into individualisation, privatisation or bureaucratisation, from the social and political issues which surround practice in the community. Perhaps the same point can be made of self-help, which needs to avoid the danger of becoming the preserve of a few relatively well-off middle-class, articulate people.

Summary

In Chapter 8, we have reviewed some of the major risks to the activities of both social workers and self-helpers, which may arise from engaging in self-help. We have acknowledged that the dangers do not run all one way, from the professional social worker to the self-helpers, but that there is a need for mutual caution in these aspects of practice. In the second part of the chapter, some ways of improving the prospects for effective relationships have been examined.

9

Furthering Self-Help

Chapter 9 is prescriptive. It brings together strands from the foregoing chapters and braids them into four major themes, first seeking to confirm the rationale for self-help and then examining the issues of values, policies and resources. Throughout, it is important to appreciate that self-help, whether integral, facilitated or autonomous, is no substitute for professional services as a whole. The following caution by Stokes has some truth, across the entire field: 'Neither self-help nor preventive health measures can relieve people of the burden of illness and death. Self-care is merely a way to gain some control over this process and to manage, not overcome, disease' (Stokes, 1981, p. 108).

Why self-help?

The rationale for self-help is that it may help people who have suffered the consequences of social or personal traumas to rebuild their confidence and hope. Knight and Hayes's comment on the inner city applies more generally:

> At present many have retreated from social action into the private world of home, family, and television, they feel powerless, and display the same signs of passivity that are sometimes found in people who have no hope, there is a need to turn this mood of oppression, anxiety, and dependency into positive action ... There are limits to what state agencies can do for inner city neighbourhoods. And since much of what they do, they do badly, there is a need to curtail some of their operations and hand them over to people who might do it better, more cheaply (Knight and Hayes, 1981, p. 95).

Previously, we have charted some of the difficulties and provided some practice illustrations and advice regarding the development of self-help. In this final chapter, this advice is drawn together in a guide to action. This is undertaken in the realisation that the field is complex and activities are various, and there is a need to restate and examine in more detail than space here permits, the values of self-help outlined in Chapter 1 and referred to in different ways in the illustrative Chapters 3–5. Further, many of the social work settings with which we are concerned leave something to be desired in terms of self-help initiatives, at least in the terms we are considering as preferable in this book. Also, it is not pretentious to suggest that social workers should be pursuing excellence and that this involves promoting innovation, challenging unthinking perpetuation of bad working practices, taking risks, and so on. Finally, there is a necessity not to miss the point of many of the self-help initiatives we have described, which is that they arise partly, if not wholly, from a dissatisfaction with professional services and from a feeling that consumers had better do something themselves.

In short, what we have surveyed is not simply a tidy, middle-class world of mutual aid. To see it that way is to miss out on the chance of learning critical lessons about the professional way of doing things for and with people. Potentially, self-help embodies opportunities for professionals to reconsider their own ways of working and change for the betterment of their clients. We shall group the points which follow in three categories: values, policies and resources.

Values

A political activity

In the latter part of the twentieth century, the words 'self-help' conjure up government cutbacks and people being expected to self-care, that is cope with their problems with minimal recourse to support from social workers and the State. While this book is being written, the map of social work services is being redrawn so as to reflect an enhanced emphasis on market competition, private provision and the voluntary sector (Griffiths, 1988). It needs to be recognised that whilst self-help may be a politically neutral concept, the contemporary social and political context makes it possible to use it to accelerate the trends just described. Or, as the illustrations of facilitated and autonomous self-help indicate, it can offer a way of challenging them.

Just because we might agree with Gladstone (1979) that a large-scale shift of resource allocation away from statutory to voluntary organisations is desirable, this is no guarantee that all the criticisms we make of the bureaucratic approach of service delivery by professionals will be no longer valid. On the contrary, the problem is social and political rather than economic, in that our values need to change so as to view the consumers of services as able to play an empowered, that is, a more active and powerful part in service delivery. The balance of power between helpers and helped, professionals and self-helpers, needs to be shifted in favour of the helped and the self-helper. The current tendency for community care to develop very unevenly throughout the country and for great unfairness to accompany the stratification of informal care to the disadvantage of women and those in the lower social classes (Ungerson, 1987, p. 153), highlights the danger of self-help becoming part of the bleak outlook for isolated, depressed and unsupported carers.

Mutual aid rather than individualism

In addressing the task of relating social work to self-help in the resource-constrained circumstances referred to, we have to remind ourselves of the rationale for encouraging self-help. It is not the emphasis on individuals pulling themselves up by their own bootstraps which appeals, but rather the centrality of mutual aid in an environment where all are encouraged to participate irrespective of their social or professional position. The most important purpose of self-help is thus not helping a smaller social work service become more cost-effective but enabling people to live a better quality life in a better society. Self-help as described in the preceding chapters points to means by which people can have a greater say in the nature and delivery of their services, either independently of, enabled by, or in partnership with, social workers. Mutual aid must be emphasised in the present social and economic climate, partly as an antidote to rampant individualism.

Professional non-professionalism and anti-professional professionalism

The divisions between the different categories and levels of self-help reviewed in Chapters 3–5 are not merely conceptual but ideological as well. Some may fit uneasily together while others will actually be incompatible. Self-help therapy and community action may thus conflict, and careful work may be needed to reconcile therapy with self-advocacy. Paradox is threaded through the whole enterprise, as indeed it is inherent in the notion of non-professional self-helpers developing an expertise in self-help which may be regarded as professional, while professionals cultivate what Parsloe referred to earlier as anti-professionalism!

Developing practice beyond a 'Western' middle-class agenda

The inclusion of the Nijeri Kori initiative in Chapter 4 redresses to a small extent the inherent ethnocentrism and Western elitism of the social work literature, as well as keeping on the agenda the need to view critically our dependence on the experience of white middle-class academia in the US, which is a feature of self-help groups as much as other aspects of social work. It also highlights the lessons we can learn from what are called Third World settings, where people often live in conditions of great political difficulty and social uncertainty and physical want. Is self-help more healthy in Thatcherite Britain in the 1980s or among the rural poor of Bangladesh?

It may be argued that self-help is a principle which will be more imaginatively and constructively employed in a social context where people are highly motivated towards, involved in, and optimistic about, grassroots politics and community action. Before undertaking new work, it will be necessary for social workers to assess local conditions in terms of the potential viability of integral or facilitated self-help in a specific area of practice.

Empowerment as a challenge to professional power and inequalities

The developments surveyed in Chapters 3–5, particularly in such areas as anti-discriminatory practice and self-advocacy, heighten the need to take seriously the efforts of people who have been on the receiving end of inadequate services to improve their self-care and the services as well! A good illustration of how to carry forward such principles through self-help is provided by the recent publication by David and Althea Brandon (1988) in the area of normalisation, emphasising that a shared goal should be allowing everybody, irrespective of their circumstances, the expectation of an ordinary way of living. A radical challenge to the structural power of the professional comes from the groups such as Survivors Speak Out referred to in Chapter 5, who challenge professional rhetoric about patient participation and consultation with clients.

This is closely allied to the notion of social workers and self-helpers treating each other as equals. There is a need to promote more real and effective sharing and co-operation among consumers and professionals. In the process, as is heralded by the forthcoming publication of the DHSS funded self-help project in Britain (Fielding, 1989, p. 7), there is a need for social workers to learn how to be both reactive and proactive. Perhaps the proactive role is a necessity for those in need of most support and help in society, in initiating the creation of mutual aid and self-care partnerships and networks.

Policies

Widening the variety and scope of social work roles

Despite their finding that self-help has little formal impact, Knight and Hayes recommend that it should be a key feature of policies to revitalise the inner cities (Knight and Hayes, 1981, p. 95), since with the right policies and resources it could be very effective. Chiefly, policy aspects include developing positive attitudes in relevant local authority departments, improving commitment by them and ensuring that co-ordination between professionals and self-helpers works effectively.

In reality, self-help may be practised within any of the three caring systems referred to on p. 126. But in practice self-help in social work crops up most frequently in the informal and voluntary sectors, to a lesser degree under the aegis of statutory bodies, while in this connection at present for all practical purposes the private sector can be discounted. Policy-wise, the following are the resource implications:

- Integral self-help involves building in to existing services
- Facilitated self-help involves stimulating innovation and more of the same elsewhere
- Autonomous self-help necessitates encouraging independence, acknowledging and demonstrating what people have, rather than presuming it is in professional workers' power to be given to them.

Enhancing the levels of social work practice

Social workers should aim to ensure that, where appropriate, a continuum of activity is encouraged, so that individual effort is not isolated from groups and the community dimension has the opportunity to influence individuals and groups.

In this respect, we may view community social work practice as in most need of development, in the light of the weaknesses indicated in Chapter 2, in the training, support and resourcing of those working in neighbourhoods alongside professional workers in social work and social care.

We can draw on experience from work with the under-fives in Chapter 3 to assert the necessity to plan on the basis of a neighbourhood-wide perception of needs and responses to them. Further, in Chapter 4, the self-build movement offers several themes we should bear in mind:

- The need for development to avoid professionals exploiting rather than empowering the poor
- The need to avoid professionals taking over activities
- The need to proceed at the pace of the consumers
- The need to keep consumers in touch with the supply of necessary resources
- Putting consumers in touch with resources.

Focussing on undervalued groups and marginalised issues

There is little doubt that the field of self-help flourishes in, among other things, areas neglected, marginalised, scorned, ignored and

undervalued by professionals. This is not accidental. Social workers should appreciate this strength of the self-help field and
encourage it accordingly, since much of the work of social workers
falls into the above category.

But the task of doing something about this is not straightforward. We can see this with reference to the experience of Asian
self-helpers in Handsworth (Chapter 5). Two issues which arise
concern the way in which social workers may promote specialist
work with, say, an Asian group and the consequences of that
initiative for the situation of Asian people in relation to the nature
and quality of their lives. We can see the argument clearly in
relation to the decision, often taken on the basis of Section 11 of
the Local Government Act 1966 funding, to employ a black
worker, specifically to work on black issues. This is how a black
worker involved in self-help in another part of Britain puts it, in an
interview for this book:

> Many black people are employed in temporary schemes or projects on
> low wages. Agencies may have obtained funds through such sources as
> Section 11 of the Local Government Act [1966]. Agencies may allocate
> to black or disabled people a quota for a reservation of places in the
> workforce. Quota or reservation policies have the advantage for
> agencies that they increase the profile of their work with undervalued
> groups in the community. But three criticisms can be made. First, there
> is often no permanence about the situation of such workers; second,
> tensions between those moving into reserved posts and other workers
> and those denied employment may have unpleasant consequences;
> third, such policies are unfair in principle because they fill gaps in the
> labour market without actually increasing overall access to the labour
> market for the people concerned . . .

> The way the Section 11 is actually employed and used by the local
> authority, the gains are all on the side of the local authority and the
> losses are on the side of the workers. The community gains but it is a
> very short-term gain and it is a very uncertain vulnerable gain . . . Black
> people are employed to work with black people. All the white
> colleagues usually offload the work. They are seen as specialist and they
> are specialist in one sense, that they do bring particular skills that social
> services does lack, but then they are expected to do the work with the
> black community. Quite often in my experience they are expected to do
> much higher level work than their colleagues would do. They are seen
> as the answer to all the white issues and represent the entire black
> community, but at the same time they are in a very vulnerable position
> which the statutory agency doesn't recognise because they have to tread
> a very thin line between the community's expectation and what the

community sees of them and what the statutory body wants them to do. And because they are on Section 11 funding it is by definition discriminatory. There are no two ways about it because they are in completely different terms and conditions and contract of employment and monetarily, than their white colleagues in mainstream employment . . .

On the service delivery side of it, the fact is that because black issues are marginalised, it's not seen as an integral part of the work. There's the work and then the black issues are attached to it and if say, for example, the black funding was actually withdrawn from the black workers then by definition the black workers would be withdrawn. Because that's the link. Black workers exist outside the structure and the community exists outside the structure and I think it's a very dangerous position to get into and therefore I think that it is very important that the work, the issues are integrated, not the people . . . In a statutory set-up the only way that you would secure the long term guarantee that the community is actually served is through integrating the issues. And also I think that all the statutory workers should be given an absolutely categorical guarantee on their work contract, that if their funding is withdrawn that they will be taken on mainstream funding. Because if the council is serious about the fact that the black work is their priority and it is the issue that's important to them, then you've got to give them the guarantee and if you give them the guarantee they can ensure that people themselves don't feel vulnerable in their jobs and that there is the long term possibility of securing service to the community, because otherwise you are in constant fear of your funding being withdrawn and you know that the minute you go, after that there's not going to be any work done, because it's the way the system works and the only way you can mitigate it is by positive steps (interview with member of Asian Self-help Group).

The above extract is worth quoting at some length because it illustrates both particular features of the situation of black people and also general aspects of self-help, in relation to the circumstances of professional social workers. Three things come across clearly: the poor bargaining position of black people, the vulnerability of their situation and their work and the tendency for crude positive discrimination to emphasise their marginalisation as individuals and groups. Rather, self-help should be part of a policy of positive action in respect of discriminated-against people.

Resources

It is a necessity to conclude this book with a re-emphasis of the issue of resources. It is the acid test of the commitment of professionals to self-help in the terms we have explored it.

The year 1989 saw the end of the DHSS-sponsored £1.75m initiative involving eighteen self-help projects in different parts of England. What long-term implications for the field of self-help does this 'pump-priming' approach to development have? What responsibility should be taken by the government and other agencies and organisations for the continued support of such activities?

Knight and Hayes (1981, p. 95) point out that insufficient funds and lack of suitable premises are key constraints on the effectiveness of self-help groups. Clearly, professionals have a role to play in ensuring that integral and facilitated activity is not stifled or impeded through such factors.

But professionals have a responsibility to phase themselves out of the picture: integral programmes perhaps should be working towards facilitation and facilitated ones towards autonomy. It is questionable whether increased resources alone can improve the circumstances of people, since often it is the professionals who benefit most from special programmes and projects (Knight and Hayes, 1981, p. 96). This leads to the conclusion that 'to ensure maximum effectiveness, resources should be allocated to those who need them with a minimum of "middle men". This suggests giving money directly to inner city residents who would be responsible for its proper use, in many cases this would involve employing local people as *indigenous workers*' (Knight and Hayes, 1981, emphasis in original).

Much of what we have argued at length above rests on different aspects of the simple but fundamental issue of *power*, chief among which are the power of the consumer to choose and the extent to which any redistribution of power between professionals and lay people is conceivable in practice.

The power to choose

Regarding the first of these, the power to choose, advice services provide an instructive alternative to a service delivery approach. In the study conducted by Knight and Hayes of thirty self-help community groups, they suggest the reason for a high level of user satisfaction may be because consumers can take the initiative and can take or leave the advice (1981, p. 94). This gives us a clue to an important principle inherent in effective self-help: namely, ensuring that consumers of social work services retain a maximum degree of control over the extent to which they receive services.

The redistribution of resources

As far as the redistribution of power between social workers and self-helpers is concerned, clearly there are some areas where it will never happen, many where it is extremely unlikely and perhaps only a few where it will be considered as possible and potentially beneficial to the interests of both parties. Translating this into resource terms, we are talking about holding the existing alloca-tion of resources in real terms and increasing it in proportion to discovered need. Where appropriate, this means not cancelling any resources removed from the professional area but transferring them to self-help.

Having said that, we need to stand back behind the resources question and set it in a broader context. What we have offered in Chapter 2 and illustrated in the subsequent three chapters, pro-vides a framework within which the existing relationships between social workers and self-helpers at least can be examined, with a view to making the most effective use of self-help principles. That is, without undermining in any way all that we have said about the crucial importance of preserving professional services, wherever it is consistent with meeting the needs of the consumers of social work services, their dependence on professional workers should be minimised. This implies looking creatively at how the fields of integral and facilitated self-help can be developed, and at how social workers should relate to autonomous self-help. It also involves increasingly making use of groups and network approaches to work with volunteers, relatives, carers, friends, neighbours, many organisations and agencies in and out of social work as well as with the local media. It involves above all not simply mobilising fresh initiatives, but tapping into what already exists in the community. It involves trying to create in oneself and in others a better understanding of the relationship between the helping acts of professionals and the helping and self-helping mechanisms which are already part of everyday life. This is an area in which there is unlikely to be a sudden enlightenment, a fanfare of trumpets and a once and for all solution. On the contrary, as in so much really useful social work, the slow and at times painful path to better practice is what counts. This book does not claim to have attained the goal, but it may make the process of working towards it somewhat more constructive and systematic.

Self-empowerment and the empowerment of practice

The most cogent argument for the development of a fuller and more effective relationship between the self-help sector and social work practice arises from the *prima facie* case to which we have pointed in this book, both for the empowerment of social workers in order that they may do the work and, even more, for the empowerment of self-helpers themselves, in furtherance of the wider aim of empowering others in the community. That is the beginning and the end of this argument for improved social work.

Summary

In Chapter 9, the final chapter, attention is paid to four more general aspects of concern to social workers in the self-help field. It deals with the rationale for self-help and social work and the issues of values, policies and resources, highlighting in the process a number of recommendations for practitioners.

Bibliography

A note follows some of the most useful references in this field for social work practitioners.

Adams, Robert (1976) 'Intermediate Treatment: Looking at Some Patterns of Intervention', *Youth Social Work Bulletin*, 3(2) (February–March) pp. 9–12.

Adams, Robert (1989) 'Parents, Children under Five and Empowerment in the Humberside Project', Humberside College of Higher Education.

Adams, Robert and Lindenfield, Gael (1985) *Self-Help and Mental Health*, Ilkley, Self-Help Associates.

Agel, Jeremy (1971) *Radical Therapist: The Radical Therapist Collective*, New York, Ballantine Books.

Altman, Dennis (1986) *AIDS and the New Puritanism*, London, Pluto Press.

Arscott, Mary-Lou *et al.* (1976) 'Alternatives in Housing? A Report on Self-Build in Britain', London, Architectural Association.

Asian Resource Centre (1987) ANNUAL REPORT 1986–87, Birmingham, Asian Resources Centre.

Audit Commission for Local Authorities in England and Wales (1986) 'Making a Reality of Community Care', A Report by the Audit Commission, London, HMSO.

Aves, G. (1969) *The Voluntary Worker in the Social Services*, London, Allen & Unwin.

Back, Kurt W. (1972) *Beyond Words: The Story of Sensitivity Training and the Encounter Movement*, New York, Russell Sage.

Bakker, Bert and Karel Mattieu (1983) 'Self-Help: Wolf or Lamb?', in Pancoast *et al.* (1983) pp. 159–81.

Balloch, Susan *et al.* (1985) *Caring for Unemployed People*, London, Bedford Square/NCVO.

Bamford, Terry (1982) *Managing Social Work*, London, Tavistock.

Bankoff, Elizabeth, A. (1979) 'Widow Groups as an Alternative to Informal Social Support', in Lieberman *et al.* (1979) pp. 181–93.

Barclay Report (1982) See Social Work, National Institute for (1982).

BASW (1984) 'Social Work in the Community', Birmingham, BASW (January 1984).

BASW (1986) 'Skills for Social Workers in the 1980s', Birmingham, BASW.

Beresford, Peter (undated) 'Patch in Perspective: Decentralising and Democratising Social Services', London, Battersea Community Action.

Beresford, Peter and Croft, Suzy (1981) 'Community Control of Social Services Departments', London, Battersea Community Action.

Birchall, Johnston (1988) *Building Communities the Co-operative Way*, London, Routledge & Kegan Paul.

Boateng, Paul (1986) 'Society and Crisis, 1984 and Beyond', in BASW (1986) pp. 3–6.

Bond, Gary R. *et al.* (1979) 'Growth of a Medical Self-Help Group', in Lieberman *et al.* (1979) pp. 43–66.

Bond, Gary R. and Reibstein, Janet (1979) 'Changing Goals in Women's Consciousness-Raising', in Lieberman *et al.* (1979) pp. 95–115.

Borman, Leonard D. (1979) 'Characteristics of Development and Growth', in Lieberman *et al.* (1979) pp. 13–42.

Borman, Leonard D. *et al.* (1982) 'Helping People to Help Themselves: Self-Help and Prevention', *Prevention in Human Services* 1(3) (Spring); the entire issue of this journal is devoted to self-help issues.

Branckaerts, Jan (1983) 'Birth of the Movement: Early Milestones', in Pancoast *et al.* (1983) pp. 143–58.

Brandon, David and Brandon, Althea (1988) *Putting People First: A Handbook on the Practical Application of Ordinary Living Principles*, London, Good Impressions; the process of self-help towards normalisation described admirably clearly and concisely in this book.

Caplan, Gerald and Killilea, Marie (1976) *Support Systems and Mutual Help: Multi-disciplinary Explorations*, New York, Grune & Stratton.

Chamberlain, Mary (1981) *Old Wives' Tales*, London, Virago.

Darvill, Giles and Munday, Brian (1984) *Volunteers in the Personal Social Services*, London, Tavistock.

Donnan, Linda and Lenton, Sue (1985) *Helping Ourselves: A Handbook for Women Starting Groups*, Toronto, Women's Press; a practical guide for self-helpers, dealing with many of the issues which arise in the setting up and running of self-help groups.

Dumont, Matthew P. (1971) *The Absurd Healer: Perspectives of a Community Psychiatrist*, New York, Viking Press.

Dumont, Matthew P. (1972) 'Revenue Sharing and the Unbuilding of Pyramids', *American Journal of Orthopsychiatry*, 42(2) (March) pp. 219–31.

Evans, Liz *et al.* (1986) *Working with Parents of Handicapped Children*, London, Bedford Square/NCVO; a useful guide to practice, arising from research monitoring a project.

Ferrand-Bechmann, Dan (1983) 'Voluntary Action in the Welfare State', in Pancoast *et al.* (1983) pp. 183–201.

Fielding, Nick (1989) 'No More Help for Self-helpers', *Community Care*, 755 (23 March) p. 7.

Gartner, Alan and Riessman, Frank (1977) *Self-Help in the Human Services*, London, Jossey-Bass.

Gartner, Alan and Riessman, Frank (1984) *The Self-Help Revolution*, New York, Human Sciences Press; a source of readings across a wide range of contemporary practice.

Gawlinski, George and Graessle, Lois (1988) *Planning Together: The Art of Effective Teamwork*, London, Bedford Square/NCVO.

Gibson, Tony (1979) *People Power: Communities and Work Groups in Action*, Harmondsworth, Penguin.

Gill, Martin and Andrews, Margaret (1987) 'Volunteers: Result Finds Volunteer Use Receives Little Priority During Training', *Social Work Today* (11 May).

Gladstone, F. J. (1979) *Voluntary Action in a Changing World*, London, Bedford Square.

Goldberg, E. M. (1966) *Welfare in the Community: Talks on Social Work to Welfare Officers*, London, Bedford Square.

Griffiths, Roy (1988) *Community Care: Agenda for Action: A Report on the Secretary of State for Social Services*, London, HMSO.

Hadley, Roger and McGrath, Morag (1980) *Going Local: Neighbourhood Social Services*, London; NCVO.

Hadley, Roger and Hatch, Stephen (1981) *Social Welfare and the Failure of the State: Centralised Social Services and Participating Alternatives*, London, Allen & Unwin.

Hadley, Roger, Dale, Peter and Sills, Patrick (1984) *Decentralising Social Services: A Model for Change*, London, NCVO.

Hadley, Roger *et al.* (1987) *A Community Social Worker's Handbook*, London, Tavistock; a practical guide, for social workers and other social services staff, to the development of community-oriented methods of social work.

Hallowitz, Emmanuel and Riessman, Frank (1967) 'The Role of the Indigenous Non-Professional in a Community Mental Health Neighbourhood', *American Journal of Orthopsychiatry*, 37, pp. 766–78.

Hatch, Stephen and Kickbusch, Ilona (eds) (1983) *Self-Help and Health in Europe: New Approaches in Health Care*, Copenhagen, World Health Organisation, Registered Office for Europe; a review of current developments in Europe under the aegis of the WHO.

Haug, Marie R. and Sussman, Marvin B. (1969) 'Professional Autonomy and the Revolt of the Client', *Social Problems*, 17, pp. 153–61.

Henderson, P. and Thomas, D. (1980) *Skills in Neighbourhood Work*, London, Allen & Unwin.

Holloway, Christine and Otto, Shirley (1986) *Getting Organised: A Handbook for Non-Statutory Organisations*, London, Bedford Square/NCVO.

Holme, Anthea and Maizels, Joan (1978) *Social Workers and Volunteers*, London, Allen & Unwin.

Howell, Elizabeth and Bayes, Marjorie (1981) *Women and Mental Health*, New York, Basic Books.

Hulke, Malcolm (ed.) (1978) *The Encyclopaedia of Alternative Medicine and Self-Help*, London, Rider & Co.; a very full reference book on the field of alternative health.

Hurvitz, Nathan (1970) 'Peer Self-Help Therapy Groups and their Implications for Psychotherapy', *Psychotherapy, Research and Practice*, 7(1) (Spring) pp. 41–9.

Hurvitz, Nathan (1974) 'Peer Self-Help Psychotherapy Groups:

Psychotherapy without Psychotherapists', in Roman and Trice (1974) pp. 84–137.

Jones, S. (1981) *Working Together: Partnerships in Local Social Service: A Working Party Report*, London, Bedford Square/NCVO.

Katz, Alfred H. (1965) 'Applications of Self-Help Concepts in Current Social Welfare', *Social Work*, 10(3) pp. 68–74.

Katz, Alfred H. (1970) 'Self-Help Organisations and Volunteer Participation in Social Welfare', *Social Work*, 15 (January) pp. 51–60.

Katz, Alfred H. and Bender, Eugene I. (1976) *The Strength in Us: Self-Help Groups in the Modern World, New Viewpoints*, New York, Franklin Watts.

Key, Michael, Hudson, Peter and Armstrong, John (1976) *Evaluation Theory and Community Work*, London, Young Volunteer Force Foundation; a source of concise guidance on issues to consider in critical appraisal.

Killilea, Marie (1976) 'Mutual Help Organisations: Interpretations in the Literature', in Caplan and Killilea (1976) pp. 37–87.

Kleiman, M. A. *et al.* (1976) 'Collaboration and Its Discontents: The Perils of Partnership', *Journal of Applied Behavioural Science*, 12, Part 3, pp. 403–10.

Knight, Barry and Hayes, Ruth (1981) *Self-Help in the Inner City*, London, London Voluntary Service Council.

Kropotkin, P. (1902) *Mutual Aid: A Factor in Evolution*, Boston, Porter Sargeant.

Kurowska, Shiela (1984) *Employing People in Voluntary Organisations*, London, Bedford Square/NCVO.

Laslett, Peter (1983) *The World We Have Lost – Further Explored*, London, Methuen.

Levy, Laureen *et al.* (1986) *Finding Our Own Solutions: Women's Experience of Mental Health Care*, London, MIND.

Levy, Leon H. (1976) 'Self-Help Groups: Types and Psychological Processes', *Journal of Applied Behavioural Science*, 12, Part 3, pp. 310–22.

Levy, Leon H. (1978) 'Self-Help Groups Viewed by Mental Health Professionals: A Survey and Comments', *American Journal of Community Psychology*, 6(4) pp. 305–13.

Levy, Leon H. (1979) 'Processes and Activities in Groups', in Lieberman *et al.* (1979) pp. 234–71.

Levy, Leo (1982) 'Mutual Support Groups in Great Britain', *Social Service in Medicine*, 16(13) pp. 1265–75.

Lieberman, Morton A. and Bond, Gary R. (1978) 'Self-Help: Problems of Measuring Outcomes', *Small Group Behaviour*, 9(2) (May) pp. 221–41.

Lieberman, Morton (1979) 'Analysing Change Mechanisms in Groups', in Lieberman *et al.* (1979) pp. 194–233.

Lieberman, Morton and Borman, Leonard D. (1976) 'Self-Help and Social Research', *Journal of Applied Behavioural Science*, 12, Part 3, pp. 455–63.

Lieberman, Morton *et al.* (1979) 'Effectiveness of Women's Consciousness Raising', in (1979) pp. 341–61.

Lieberman, Morton *et al.* (1979) *Self-Help Groups for Coping with Crisis: Origins, Members, Processes and Impact*, San Francisco, Jossey Bass; a compendium of research in the US which is dated but relevant.

Lindenfield, Gael and Adams, Robert (1984) *Problem Solving through Self-Help Groups*, Ilkley, Self-Help Associates.

Lurie, Harry (ed.) (1965) *Encyclopaedia of Social Work*, National Association of Social Workers.

Marieskind, Helen I. (1984) 'Women's Self-Help Groups', in Gartner and Riessman (1984) pp. 27–32.

Moeller, Michael L. (1983) 'Self-Help and the Medical Practitioner', in Hatch and Kickbusch (eds) (1983) pp. 68–76.

Mowrer, O. Hobart (1964) *The New Group Therapy*, Princeton, Van Nostrand.

Mowrer, O. Hobart (1972) 'Integrity Groups: Principles and Procedures', *The Counselling Psychologist*, 3, pp. 7–33.

Mowrer, O. Hobart (1984) 'The Mental Health Professions and Mutual Help Programs: Co-optation or Collaboration?', in Gartner and Riessman (1984) pp. 139–54.

Norman, Janet (1976) 'Consciousness-Raising: Self-Help in the Women's Movement', in Katz and Bender (1976) Chapter 16.

Pancoast, Diane L., Parker, Paul and Froland, Charles (1983) *Rediscovering Self-Help: Its Role in Social Care*, Beverly Hills, Sage; a collection of papers reviewing international self-help practice.

Parsloe, Phyllida (1986) 'What Skills do Social Workers Need?', in BASW (1986) pp. 7–15.

Patton, Michael Quinn (1982) *Practical Evaluation*, Beverley Hills, Sage.

Payne, Malcolm (1986) *Social Care in the Community*, London, Macmillan.

Preston-Shoot, Michael (1987) *Effective Groupwork*, London, BASW/ Macmillan.

Riessman, Frank (1965) 'The "Helper" Therapy Principle', *Social Work*, 10 (April).

Richardson, Ann (1983) 'English Self-Help: Varied Patterns and Practices', in Pancoast *et al.* (1983) pp. 203–21.

Richardson, Ann (1984) *Working with Self-Help Groups: A Guide for Local Professionals*, London, Bedford Square/NCVO.

Richardson, Ann and Goodman, Meg (1983) *Self-Help and Social Care: Mutual Aid Organisations in Practice*, London, Policy Studies Institute; a study of four national associations, highlighting practice issues.

Robinson, David and Henry, Stuart (1977) *Self-Help and Health: Mutual Aid for Modern Problems*, London, Martin Robertson.

Roman, Paul, M. and Trice, Harrison M. (1974) *The Sociology of Psychotherapy*, New York, Jason Aronson.

Rowbotham, Sheila *et al.* (1980) *Beyond the Fragments: Feminism and the Making of Socialism*, London, Merlin.

Sarachild, Kathie (1971) 'Consciousness-Raising and Intuition', in Agel (1971).

Sarbin, Theodore R. (1971) 'Self-Reconstitution Processes: A Preliminary Report', *Psychoanalytic Review*, 57(4) pp. 599–615.

Satyamurti, Carole (1981) *Occupational Survival: The Case of the Local Authority Social Worker*, Oxford: Basil Blackwell.

Sidel, Victor W. and Sidel, Ruth (1976) 'Beyond Coping', *Social Policy*, (September–October) pp. 67–9.

Silverman, Phyllis R. (1980) *Mutual Help Groups: Organisation and Development*, Beverly Hills, Sage.

Social Work, National Institute for (1982) *Social Workers, Their Role and Tasks (The Barclay Report)*, London, Bedford Square.

Smiles, Aileen (1956) *Samuel Smiles and his Surroundings*, London, Robert Hale.

Smiles, Samuel (1875) *Thrift*, London, Harper & Bros.

Smiles, Samuel (1890) *Self-Help; With Illustrations of Conduct and Perseverence*, London, John Murray.

Stokes, Bruce (1981) *Helping Ourselves: Local Solutions to Global Problems*, London, Norton.

Tax, Sol (1976) 'Self-Help Groups: Thoughts on Public Policy', *Journal of Applied Behavioural Science*, 12, Part 3, pp. 448–54.

Toren, Nina (1972) *Social Work: The Case of a Semi-Profession*, Beverley Hills, Sage.

Townsend, Peter (1979) *Poverty in the United Kingdom*, London, Allen & Unwin.

Tracy, George S. and Gussow Zachary (1976) 'Self-Help Groups: A Grassroots Response to a Need for Services', *Journal of Applied Behavioural Science*, 12, Part 3, pp. 381–96.

Twelvetrees, Alan (1982) *Community Work*, London, BASW/Macmillan.

Tyler, Ralph W. (1976) 'Social Policy and Self-Help Groups', *Journal of Applied Behavioural Science*, 12, Part 3, pp. 444–8.

Unell, Judith (1987) *Help for Self-Help: A Study of a Local Support Service*, London, Bedford Square/NCVO.

Ungerson, Clare (1987) *Policy is Personal: Sex, Gender and Informal Care*, London, Tavistock.

Vattano, Anthony J. (1972) 'Power to the People: Self-Help Groups', *Social Work*, 17(4) (July) pp. 7–15.

Videka, Lynn M. (1979) 'Psychosocial Adaptation in a Medical Self-Help Group', in Lieberman *et al.* (1979) pp. 362–86.

Wates, Nick and Kwevitt, Charles (1987) *Community Architecture: How People are Creating Their Own Environment*, Harmondsworth, Penguin.

Webb, Penny (1982) 'Back to Self-Help?', *Royal Society of Health Journal*, 102, Part 3 (June) pp. 124–9.

Wechsler, Henry (1960) 'The Self-Help Organisation in the Mental Health Field: Recovery Inc. A Case Study', *Journal of Nervous and Mental Diseases*, 130, pp. 297–314.

Willen, Mildred L. 'Parents Anonymous: The Professional's Role as Sponsor', in Gartner and Riessman (1984) pp. 109–19.

Wilson, Judy (1988) *Caring Together: Guidelines for Carers' Self-Help and Support Groups*, London, King's Fund; advice and information on starting or becoming involved in a carers' group.

Wilson, Judy (1986) *Self-Help Groups: Getting Started – Keeping Going*, Harlow, Longman.

Wilson, Melba (1989) 'Overcoming the Legacy of Child Sexual Abuse', *Social Work Today*, 20(30) pp. 12–13.

Wolfenden, Lord (1978) *The Future of Voluntary Organisations: Report of the Wolfenden Committee*, London, Croom Helm.

Woolley, Tom (ed.) (1985) *The Characteristics of Community Architecture and Community Technical Aid*, Occasional Paper, No. 85/6, Glasgow, University of Strathclyde.

Young, Michael and Rigge, Marianne (undated) *Mutual Aid in a Selfish Society: A Plea for Strengthening the Co-operative Movement*, Paper No. 2, London, Mutual Aid Press.

Zweig, Marilyn (1971) 'Is Women's Liberation a Therapy Group?', in Agel (1971).

Index